Lost Stories of the Great War

ROSALIE LAUERMAN

Lost Stories
OF THE
Great War

To Dave, Kurt, and Tom
Thank you for your unwavering support

Front cover image: Back Our Girls Over There. Clarence Frederick Underwood, 1918
Courtesy Young Women's Christian Association via
Library of Congress, Prints and Photographs, LC-USZC4-1421

Back cover image: Our Regular Divisions. James Montgomery Flagg, 1918
Courtesy Library of Congress, Prints and Photographs, LC_USZC4-10225

Frontis piece image: President Woodrow Wilson, Official Presidential Portrait
Frank Graham Cootes, 1913. Courtesy Everett Historical/Shutterstock.com

Cover and interior design by Lilian Rosenstreich

Copyright: © 2019, Rosalie Lauerman, all rights reserved
Published by Rosalie Lauerman, rosalielauerman@msn.com
ISBN: 978-0-692-08224-9

Acknowledgements

For significant contributions to "Lost Stories," I gratefully recognize the following: Carol Gaskin for her thorough and precise edits; Lilian Rosenstreich for the outstanding creative design and layout of "Lost Stories;" Paul Violette, President and Curator of the New Hampshire Telephone Museum, for his expertise; Karen Clarkson for her delightful Native American art; Mike Constandy of Westmoreland Research for clear and crisp imagery; Kimberly Kenney, Curator of the McKinley Presidential Library and Museum, for rare quotes; and Andrea Laws at the University Press of Kansas, for vital quotes. And above all, I appreciate and value the enthusiastic encouragement and support of family and friends.

Contents

Introduction	9	MAPS	
ONE The Great War	11	European Alliances 1914	10
TWO Telephone Linemen	25	Western Front 1914–1918	33
THREE Hello Girls	39	Lost Battalion 1918	77
FOUR Fighting 8th	51	European Borders 1919	120
FIVE Code Talkers	65		
SIX Carrier Pigeons	73	EXPLORE	
SEVEN Combat Artists	87	Timeline	126
EIGHT Flying Schoolgirls	99	Museums, Media, and Books	129
NINE Peace	113	Educator Resources	132
		Source Notes	133
		Selected Bibliography	138

Introduction

You may recall that the Great War—now known as World War One—was a conflict that erupted one hundred years ago in Europe over territory and power. It raged for four years and engulfed more than twenty countries around the globe. It was the first war where battles involved armored tanks, machine guns, barbed wire, poison gas, long-range artillery guns, submarines, and military airplanes. The Great War changed the world and the way wars would be fought forevermore.

This collection of authentic stories uncovers ordinary people carrying out extraordinary deeds. Their narrative reveals acts of courage, strength, patriotism, and persistence. One cannot help but find these determined men, women, and even a small bird inspiring.

And hopefully, we'll always remember them and retell their stories.

Allies Day, May 1917. **Childe Hassam, 1917, Oil on canvas. Patriotism overflowed in New York City when America entered World War I. A flurry of English, French, and American flags proudly waved above parades on Fifth Avenue. The artist dedicated this painting to the coming together of nations to fight for democracy.** Courtesy National Gallery of Art/Everett Art/Shutterstock.com.

European military alliances 1914. The tan countries were neutral. Italy switched it's alliance from the Central Powers to the Allied Powers in 1915. Courtesy Wikimedia Commons.

ONE
The Great War

"On the eve of the outbreak of the war there were six great powers in the world and a cluster of smaller ones, each armed to the teeth and straining every nerve to get ahead of the others in deadliness of equipment and military efficiency;" H. G. Wells wrote in his novel, The War in the Air, *published six years before the Great War broke out.*

A chain of events with echoes around the globe swept through Europe in the summer of 1914. At the time, the map of Europe looked quite different from how it looks today. The European countries, including Germany, France, Austria-Hungary, and others, quarreled over territorial boundaries, naval dominance, power, and **alliances.**

Germany, a young country with a growing economy and a modern army, envied the glory of superpowers like its neighbors, Britain and France, with their wealth of colonies. In 1914 most of the European nations were bulking up the size and strength of their armies. Germany and Britain were racing to build the most powerful navy.

The tension climaxed on June 28, 1914. Archduke Franz Ferdinand, heir to the throne of Austria-Hungary, and his wife Sophie were in the Bosnian City of Sarajevo to attend a ceremonial army review. When their open car stopped, an enraged Serbian revolutionary stepped up and shot

An alliance is a group of nations coming together to achieve a common goal. Each country within the group is called an ally.

the archduke and Sophie. She died instantly; the archduke bled to death shortly after. The revolutionary was captured and arrested.

The assassination triggered a series of escalating events that led to a world at war.

- July 28, 1914. Austria-Hungary declared war on Serbia to retaliate for the archduke's murder.
- July 29. Austria-Hungary attacked the Serbian city of Belgrade, located near the Austria-Hungary border.
- Russia allied with Serbia because the two countries shared a common language, religion, and culture. Russia began mobilizing—assembling and preparing troops and supplies for war. This worried Germany because Russia and Germany shared a long border. In the interest of self-defense, Germany began marshalling its own military.
- August 1. Germany declared war on Russia in support of Austria-Hungary, in keeping with a secret 1881 treaty in which Germany and Austria-Hungary pledged to support each other in wartime.
- August 3. Germany declared war on France, based on the Schlieffen Plan of 1897. The plan spelled out a strategy to invade and conquer France quickly, then take on Russia. It proposed invading small, neutral Belgium to get to France.
- August 4. The German Army marched into Belgium, demanding passage through that neutral country so it could capture its ultimate goal, Paris, the French capital. To Germany's surprise, Belgium resisted.
- August 4. The United Kingdom of Great Britain, commonly called Britain, declared war against Germany. Britain and Belgium had signed a treaty agreeing that Britain would help Belgium defend its neutrality if invaded.
- Mid-August. France, Britain, and Serbia declared war on Germany. Austria-Hungary declared war on Russia.

Alliance of Powers in the Great War

CENTRAL POWERS	ALLIED POWERS
Germany	United Kingdom and Commonwealth
Austria-Hungary	France and Colonies
Ottoman Empire (Turkey)	Russia (1914-1917)
Bulgaria (1916-1918)	Belgium
	Serbia
	Italy (1915-1918)
	Japan
	Romania (1916-1918)
	Greece (1917-1918)
	United States (1917-1918)
	Others

Data courtesy US Army Center of Military History, www.history.army.mil/HTML/Bookshelves/Resmat/WWI/

Germany found itself simultaneously at war with Russia, France, Great Britain, Belgium, and Serbia—a situation completely beyond the scope of the Schlieffen Plan. All of Europe was plunged into a violent war that no one really wanted. Each country believed it had been forced into the inferno by the actions of another country.

The colonies of the vast European empires around the globe were also drawn into the war—as well as other small countries. With so many nations at war, the conflict was labeled the World War or the Great War, and at its conclusion, the War to End All Wars. The public believed that the Great War had been so brutal that no one would ever wage war on such a scale again. (Unfortunately, the Great War did not end all wars. After World War Two erupted just twenty years later, the Great War became known as World War One and the First World War.)

In 1914 the United Kingdom of Great Britain included England, Scotland, Ireland, and Wales. Realizing that its forces were too small to take on the Central Powers, Britain also called for volunteers from its vast Empire of colonies—Australia, Canada, India, New Zealand, Newfoundland, South Africa, and others.

THE GREAT WAR

Spotlighting Technology

New technologies invented and used during the Great War had an enormous impact on how that war was fought and how future wars would be fought. The Great War is often considered the first truly modern war. In addition to telephones and radios, the following innovations quickly became vital to the infantrymen.

MACHINE GUNS enabled infantry to fire continuous rounds of ammunition rapidly. The rapid-firing guns drove infantrymen to dig trenches and dive into them to avoid being shot to pieces.

ARTILLERY GUNS, cannons, and other heavy guns evolved to offset the effects of machine guns. They fired larger shells that traveled farther distances than machine-gun fire. Artillery gunners poured their firepower on the enemy to pin them down and allow their own army to advance. A German howitzer cannon with a 16.5-inch barrel, called "Big Bertha," was the most powerful cannon at the time.

MOTORIZED ARMORED TANKS were developed to break out of the stalled war in the trenches. Tanks were self-propelled, bulletproof, accommodated one or more guns, moved on caterpillar tracks, and housed a two-man crew. Tanks flattened barbed wire, rolled over trenches and shell craters, and climbed muddy hillsides. This French tank is a Renault FT-17.

AIRPLANES, only a decade old, were small and fragile at the beginning of the war. Originally used for observation, the airplane emerged from the war as the most significant military weapon of the future. With a machine gun mounted up front, it became a fighter plane. Bombers were developed to fly long distances carrying heavy bombs. The photo shows a French Nieuport 27.

Following the Schlieffen Plan, Germany declared war on Belgium on August 4, 1914, and stormed the defensive forts around the city of Liège. The smaller Belgian Army fought back. In response, the German Army wheeled in its heaviest howitzer cannons, called "Big Berthas." The soldiers said that the Big Berthas were worse than the "mouth of hell."

The howitzers smashed the steel and concrete forts into piles of rubble. They crushed the overwhelmed Belgian soldiers into oblivion. The last of Belgium's forts surrendered on August 17, and Germany occupied the country from 1914 to 1918. On their march through Belgium, the German Army terrorized the Belgian citizens and set fire to their villages. Forty thousand ravaged Belgian refugees fled their country, leaving their homes, their gardens, and most of their possessions behind.

Chaplain William Braddan with the 93rd Division, U.S. Army, wrote in his memoirs:

> *Homes that required a life-time to possess are left tearfully behind. Gardens filled with everything from strawberries to potatoes, great*

Belgian refugees flee their country ahead of invading German Army.
Courtesy Wikimedia Commons.

fields of grain, ripe to harvest, are all left—spade left sticking in the half-upturned sod, everything left—all moving back of the zone of fire.

The victorious Germans boldly marched into France on August 23, 1914. They shoved the British and French Armies back, deeper and deeper toward France's capital, Paris. Germany fought to capture Paris in accordance with their grand plan. The Germans believed that if they bombed the "City of Light" and blasted its cathedrals and museums into ruins, the French people would despair and surrender.

In early September 1914, German and Allied troops fought a high-stakes battle called the First Battle of the Marne. The Marne River is a 319-mile tributary of the Seine River east of Paris. The Allies fought to save Paris; the Germans fought to carry out the Schlieffen plan. The German Army reached the outskirts of Paris. But after five days of battling, the allied French and British armies had stopped the enemy's troops and pushed them back to the French border. About half a million Allied and Central Powers troops were killed or wounded in the First Battle of the Marne.

The German Army dug trenches near the Aisne River in northeastern France. The Allied Armies dug in too. For the next three years the faceoff was stalled in a continuous war from the trenches along a stabilized front line. Neither side could find a way to break out of the bloody stalemate. The front line rarely moved. The killing continued.

Trench warfare became a necessary survival measure. The trenches, six feet wide and seven feet deep, protected the men, their equipment, and supplies. Soldiers on each side of the fighting front lived in trenches dug along the 470-mile battlefront.

The soldiers called the wasteland between the Allies' and the Central Powers' trenches No Man's Land for good reason—men died there. The width of No Man's Land varied from a few hundred feet to about a mile. The treach-

American soldiers in camouflaged trench at the front line during the Meuse-Argonne Offensive.
Courtesy Everett Historical/Shutterstock.com.

erous strip was riddled with shell craters, burnt tree stumps, and snarls of barbed wire—a twisted steel wire with embedded sharp points, or barbs, originally designed to fence in cattle. During the war, both the Allies and the Central Powers coiled barbed wire throughout No Man's Land to snarl enemy attackers.

A Scots officer described the deplorable conditions in the trenches:

> *No one who was not there can fully appreciate the excruciating agonies and misery through which the men had to go… Paddling about by day, sometimes with water above their knees; standing at night, hour after hour on sentry duty, while the drenched boots, puttees [cloth wrapped tightly around the leg for support] and breeches [pants] became stiff like cardboard with ice from the freezing cold air.*

Robert Graves, a British captain, described his first day in the trenches in his autobiography, as follows:

> *A German flare shot up, broke into bright flame, dropped slowly and went hissing into the grass just behind our trench, showing up the bushes and pickets. Instinctively I moved. 'It's bad to do that, sir,' he [the night sentry] said, as a rifle bullet cracked and seemed to pass right between us. 'Keep still, sir, and they can't spot you.'*

Rats, frogs, slugs, beetles, fleas, flies, and lice lived in the trenches and spread diseases. Snipers fired at any visible movement in the enemy's trenches. The air reeked of dead bodies. Trenches were often filled with knee-deep mud. Despite the conditions, digging in was vital for survival. Britain issued more than ten million shovels to the troops.

The spring of 1917 was the lowest point of the war for the French troops. They had just lost tens of thousands of men during the Second Battle of the Aisne, in northeastern France. Most French households grieved over the loss or wounding of a loved one. Rumors spread that the French were disheartened and that Germany was preparing for a massive drive toward Paris.

A trio of newly-arrived American Expeditionary Forces (AEF) soldiers observed a train returning from the front. One soldier described the train:

> *The train was a hospital train. ... We could look directly in through the windows of the train as it moved slowly past us. It was packed with men. Men lying as still as if they were already dead. Men shaking with pain. One man raving, jabbering, yelling, in delirium. Everywhere bandages ... bandages ... bandages ... and blood. It shook me up badly. And yet I couldn't seem to stop looking at it.*

The Second Battle of the Ainse and the resulting casualties demoralized the French troops. Mutiny reared its ugly head. After three years of trench life, some abandoned their posts and refused to return to the trenches. By the beginning of June about 35,000 men were involved in various mutinies. More than half of the French divisions were infected with clusters of mutineers. It was bound to spread.

The men objected to foul conditions in the trenches, lack of leave time, and inferior food. But mostly, they were concerned about the welfare of their families, as leave times were frequently canceled. They were not protesting about their officers or the war itself. Despair motivated their actions.

General Henri-Philippe Pétain, commander of the French armies in the

A Red Cross Train, France. **Harold Septimus Power, 1918. Transferring wounded soldiers from an ambulance to a Red Cross Train.** Courtesy H. Septimus Power via Wikimedia Commons.

northeast, addressed the situation with restraint. He understood that his soldiers had endured the trenches for three years and needed a break. He understood that they needed leave time to go home and confirm that their families were okay.

General Pétain ordered a temporary halt to further offensives, granted rest and leave time as earned, and ordered proper beds for the barracks behind the lines. The general punished the worst offenders. He attempted to revive his soldiers' patriotism. And no doubt, Pétain hoped young, fresh Americans would join the fight before it was too late.

By the end of July, most of the infantrymen were back at their posts. The German government didn't know about the mutinies; that information was kept top-secret for decades.

Meanwhile, a few countries around the globe remained neutral during the war; they did not take sides. The United States remained neutral even when in 1915 a German submarine sank the Lusitania, a British luxury ocean liner. Although 1,198 innocent passengers drowned—including more than one hundred Americans—the American people considered it an isolated event and were not ready to go to war.

Three major incidents in 1917 changed the mind of most Americans, however, when they began to see Germany as the aggressor.

1. January 16. Germany declared unrestricted submarine warfare and threatened to sink all ships that entered the war zone, even if they were neutral.

2. February 28. News media released a secret telegram that Germany had sent to Mexico, proposing that Mexico join with Germany and attack the U.S. to gain additional territory.

3. March 18. The U.S. learned that German submarine torpedoes sank three American commercial ships. The ships were clearly identified as vessels belonging to U.S. corporations. The oil tanker, the Illinois, was one of the ships sunk by the torpedoes. It was homeward bound, had "U.S.A." painted on its side, and was flying two large U.S. flags.

Iconic Uncle Sam recruiting poster. James Montgomery Flagg, 1917. Courtesy Library of Congress Prints and Photographs, LC-DIG-ppmsc-03521 via Dover Publications, Inc.

President Wilson reluctantly called a special session of Congress on April 2, 1917. He had hoped for "peace among equals," but now he and most Americans believed that Germany's cause was ethically and morally wrong. In his speech to Congress, the president warned that "The world must be made safe for democracy." He urged Congress to declare war against Germany. Four days later the Senate and House of Representatives voted to wage war against Germany's aggression.

And so, almost three years after the Great War had begun, the United States joined the Allied battle against the aggression of the Central Powers. In the beginning, officials and most Americans believed that the Allies needed war materials, funding, and food. Later they learned that what the Allies needed most was fresh manpower to add to their dwindling supply of young men.

At the time, the U.S. Army totaled 400,000 troops—regular soldiers and National Guardsmen—with scant training and experience. When they arrived in France, French officers taught them battlefield tactics and trench warfare skills.

At home, the United States began building up its army through recruitment posters, pamphlets, and other advertising urging eligible men to enlist. By war's end the U.S. had mobilized four million troops for the Great War, half of whom served in Europe.

General John J. Pershing was appointed Commander of the American Expeditionary Force, called the AEF. He was a competent and experienced general. But would the young, untested U.S. Army be able to make a difference?

Spotlighting War Gardens

When fighting in Europe erupted in 1914, people around the globe began experiencing severe food shortages. Many in Europe were starving because their farmers were fighting at the frontlines. To combat famine, Americans were encouraged to plant vegetables in their backyards, public parks, and vacant lots. The patriotic plots were called War Gardens. The National War Garden Commission launched a campaign of press releases, posters, and leaflets explaining how to turn empty land into vegetable patches and how to preserve surplus produce.

U.S. schoolchildren aged nine to fifteen were encouraged to plant School Gardens. The young gardeners dutifully tended their produce in backyards and nearby vacant lots on Saturdays and after school. The School Garden Army aimed to teach thrift, industry, service, patriotism, and responsibility. Because so many Americans cultivated War Gardens and School Gardens, food supplies expanded, waste was reduced, and more food was available for the troops in Europe. War Gardens were a major success.

TWO
Telephone Linemen

A French officer marveled at American efficiency, saying, "In the morning the Americans get a concession to build a telephone line; in the afternoon, there is a hole; by night there is a pole; the next morning there is a wire; and by night there is a message."

General John J. Pershing arrived in France on June 13, 1917 and was warmly welcomed. He found the war locked in a bloody stalemate with neither side able to gain new territory, and yet the killing continued. He wanted to be in the thick of the fighting so, after inspecting several sites, he established the American Expeditionary Force (AEF) headquarters in Chaumont, about 170 miles northeast of Paris, France.

The French celebrated the arrival of General Pershing and 14,000 U.S. Army troops from the 1st Division. The people were overjoyed, grateful, and welcoming. These young, fresh, American troops would fight alongside their husbands, sons, and brothers. They would help save Paris. To honor the event, the French government organized a Fourth of July parade through Paris.

Military Telephone Linemen at Work Under Enemy Shell Fire. Courtesy Scientific American Magazine, March 23, 1918.

The parade stopped at the tomb of the Marquis de Lafayette. General Pershing solemnly laid a wreath of roses on the tomb and stepped back. Lieutenant Colonial Charles Stanton was designated to deliver the address. Stanton concluded his speech with a rousing "Lafayette, we are here!" It was a clear statement that the Americans have come to repay Lafayette's contributions toward winning the American Revolution in 1776.

As Pershing settled in at headquarters, he discovered that the already un-

General John J. Pershing, Commander of the American Expeditionary Force, 1919. George Grantham Bain, publisher. Courtesy Library of Congress via Wikimedia Commons.

derstaffed and overloaded French telephone system was not nearly as dependable as the U.S. telephone system he relied on back home.

The American commander concluded that, to be effective, the army must have a reliable telephone network. They needed the newest technology—telephone and telegraph services on an American scale. So he had a complete and up-to-the-minute American telephone and telegraph system transported from the United States to France through submarine-infested waters. Although the system was modern and ingenious, its use was risky. The success or failure of the war could hinge on the effectiveness of its communications system—and no one could be sure the system would work in a war zone.

Pershing also required that experienced U.S. telephone technicians and linemen be used to install and maintain the new system in Europe. The army recruited the best cable splicers, linemen, installers, and mechanics. They were assigned to the U.S. Army Signal Corps, where they would design, construct, maintain, and operate all communication systems.

A team of Signal Corps linemen was assigned to each combat battalion and charged with keeping their battalion's telephone lines working. In fighting zones, telephone and telegraph lines were installed by fastening wires to tree branches, bushes, fenceposts, whatever was at hand. Linemen worked in spite of enemy fire and bad weather. Many times lines were laid on the ground or wrapped around insulated crossbars on short poles. The low poles were easier to repair and less visible than tall poles.

The thin wires broke easily under the impact of enemy shelling, heavy artillery traffic, and careless footsteps. To repair a break during combat, linemen rushed out, hauling forty pounds of wire as well as their packs and weapons. As quickly as

TELEPHONE LINEMEN

The U.S. Army Signal Corps began in 1860 with responsibility for new technologies. In addition to telegraph, telephone, and radio communications systems, the 1917 Signal Corps included visual signaling with flags and torches, hot-air balloons, combat photography, military weather service, and more.

possible they traced the location of the break and spliced the wire back together, usually ducking bullets.

One telephone lineman described his first days on the job:

We were chasing all the uniforms we saw all over the country, with a coil of duplex [wire] in a wheelbarrow, hoping they would settle in one place long enough for us to give them some telephone service.

The U.S. 26th Division, nicknamed the "Yankee Division" or "Yanks," was one of the first divisions of the AEF (American Expeditionary Force) to arrive in France. They joined French troops at the tiny hamlet of Seicheprey, France, about fourteen miles east of St. Mihiel.

At Seicheprey, German Stormtroopers with flame-throwers led the attack. As they progressed through the town, Allied troops fell back and suffered heavy casualties. But the Allies regained Seicheprey by late afternoon. In the end they hadn't lost any ground.

Boston Globe war correspondent Frank Palmer Sibley traveled with the Yankee Division. Sibley knew many of the soldiers and considered himself a member of the unit. He always referred to the unit as "we." He reported this action at Seicheprey on April 20, 1918:

[We received] the most intense artillery fire the Division had seen up to that time. As usual, the first thing that happened to us was the cutting of our telephone lines. The signalmen went out and repaired them; as fast as the lines were mended they were cut again. These boys worked all day and all night under the shells, tracing and repairing breaks in the wires with a courage whose magnificence can hardly be understood.

The Germans considered Seicheprey a brief raid designed to show that the Americans were weak and inexperienced. The Allies considered it a victory.

The British and the French were hoping that fresh Americans would be used to reinforce the gaps their units, but Pershing resisted. He wanted to use the American Expeditionary Force as a single unit under his command. At that moment, however, the German Army was boldly marching to Paris. If they captured Paris, the French would be demoralized and the war would end in a Germany victory.

After General Pershing realized what was at stake, he agreed to loan France the AEF 1st Division, a large, experienced, and proud unit. He also saw that the Allied effort needed more men quickly. U.S. troops continued to arrive in France throughout the war. More than four million American men were mobilized for the Great War; half went to France.

On May 28, 1918, French, British, and AEF troops prepared to fight side by side at Cantigny, a small agricultural village about sixty miles straight north of Paris. At 4:45 AM Allied guns began the attack.

Oscar A. Bondelid, an experienced telephone technician assigned to an AEF Signal Corps detachment, described his experience during the battle at Cantigny:

> *The enemy got pretty busy with their artillery and the [telephone] line went out of order. My corporal and I went out to fix it and were gone over two hours. As fast as the line could be repaired in one place it would be broken in another. But by a lot of hard work we finally managed to patch it up. ... In all, eight pieces of high explosives found their way into various parts of my clothing and body.*

Bondelid was cited for "Conspicuous gallantry in action."

Massive French guns lit up the sky for miles. By 7:20 AM the battle was over, and the Allies had taken Cantigny. The Americans showed the Germans, French, British, and especially themselves that AEF troops could fight and win.

The AEF faced its first major offensive at St. Mihiel, about ninety miles east of Château-Thierry along the frontline. The mission was to recapture

French territory that Germany had seized in 1914. AEF troops, reinforced by French artillery, attacked on September 12, 1918. Thirteen divisions of the American Expeditionary Force and eight French divisions, totaling 264,000 men, began a well-planned attack against 75,000 Germans. Almost three thousand artillery pieces bombarded the enemy for four hours.

Major Nels Anderson, Signal Corps Wire Chief, described the job of keeping battlefield communications working at St. Mihiel:

> *The St. Mihiel affair was a veritable nightmare for the telephone men in the artillery. After the first jump-off we were advancing so rapidly that it was nearly impossible to maintain communication; and at no time was it more important. We would advance to a new position,*

Signal Corps soldier unreels telephone wire. Courtesy National Archives.

and just about the time we had communication we would advance again.

We were getting lots of gas, the masks had to be worn almost continually. I would like to put a gas mask on you sometime, and then have you try to talk over a telephone, then make a dash across country for a mile or so with somebody throwing brickbats at you at every jump, and then try to splice a wire. This would give you some idea of the ordinary work which we had to go through with.

Poison gas as a chemical weapon was introduced during the Great War. Poisonous gas was released into the air and formed a cloud over the troops. Exposure to tear gas, mustard gas, and chlorine gas can burn skin, irritate eyes and throats, and cause choking. Gas masks were quickly developed and used to reduce the effects of chemical weapons.

After battling for thirty hours, the outnumbered Germans relinquished the contested area. The successful mission at St. Mihiel revived Allies' spirits and boosted the Americans' confidence.

General Pershing hurried his troops to the Meuse-Argonne sector, where the Allies planned a series of coordinated offensive actions involving all Allied Armies. The troops lined up along the entire length of the 470-mile Western Front which stretched from the Belgian coast in the north to the Swiss border in the south. American units were assigned the Meuse-Argonne sector with Allied Armies alongside them.

Private John W. Nell, an infantryman with the 77th Division, described the Argonne Woods in his memoir as follows:

Considering the masses of barb wire entanglements, and a modern trench system, along with the terrain being heavily wooded, with immensely thick underbrush, rugged hills, deep narrow ravines, and marshy valleys covered with heavy growth of briars, vines and brush,

British soldier and horse wearing gas masks. The ghoulish-looking masks were uncomfortable and dehumanizing but essential.
Courtesy Science Photo Library.

this was no place to engage the enemy. To advance through this section was nearly impossible.

But now Private Nell and the rest of the AEF, more than one million U.S. soldiers under General Pershing's command, faced this nearly impossible advance. On September 26, 1918, the combined Allied forces surged forward across the entire length of the Western Front. The Americans' goal was to capture the railway hub at Sedan, a main German supply line. The slaughter raged for forty-seven days and stopped only when all the combatants agreed to a cease-fire on

November 11, 1918. The Meuse-Argonne offensive was the AEF's largest battle of the war and the bloodiest battle in American history at that time.

During the Argonne offensive, linemen exceeded expectations to keep the communications system working. One lineman, Sergeant Ernest Toppel, was running telephone wire along the frontlines on October 13, 1918, when he was wounded in the back by shrapnel. The next day, while making his way to the aid station, he received another shrapnel wound to his right leg. The United States awarded the sergeant a Silver Star for displaying exceptional bravery as a member of a wire-carrying party, who "advanced repeatedly under heavy shell and machine gun fire to open up communications."

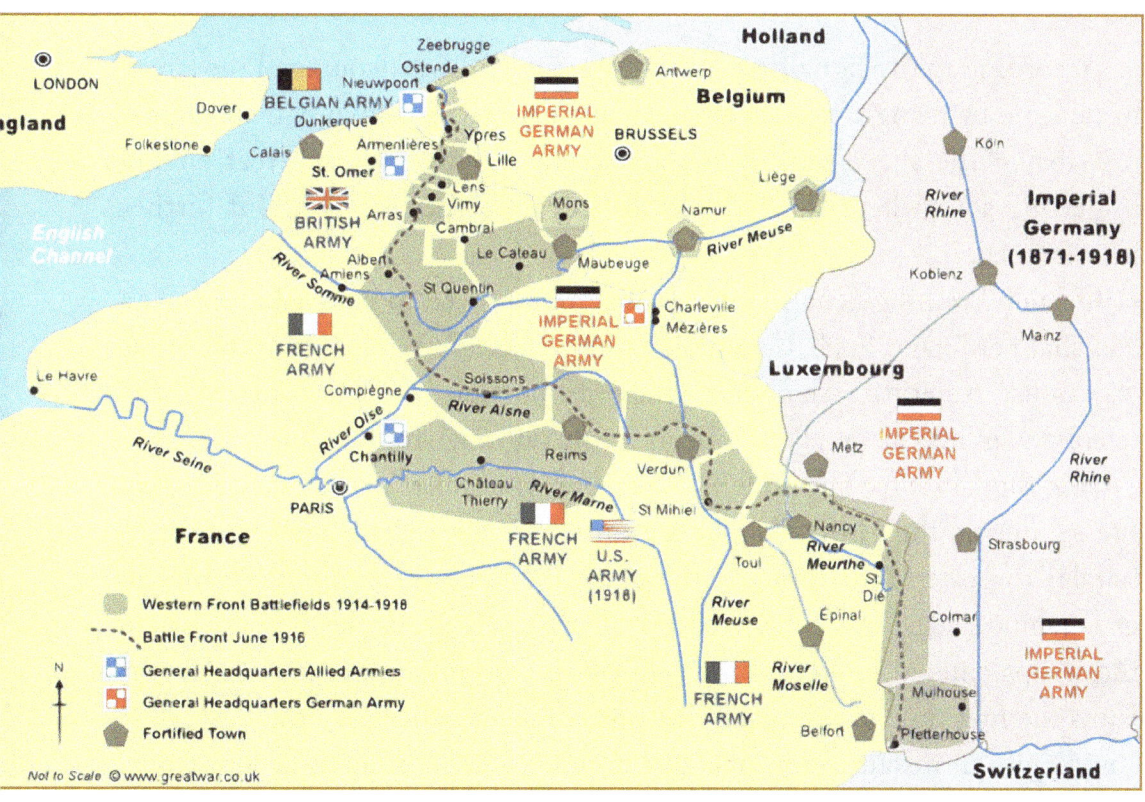

Western Front 1914-1918. *Map shows the major battlefields along the Western Front.* Courtesy Wikimedia Commons.

Sometimes, keeping the lines humming could be humorous, like this signalman's report:

> *One fine, clear, frosty day in the midst of firing, Observation Post No. 8 was reported out of communication. ... On arriving at a point where the wires crossed a natural meadow, the signal officer was greatly surprised to find a flock of sheep busily engaged in eating the insulation off the telephone wires. ... They had removed the insulation from about one hundred yards of wire in a very thorough manner and had crossed and tangled the circuits so that it was impossible to clear them.*

According to the signalman, a nearby artillery unit encouraged the sheep to relocate by firing a few shots over their heads. The signalman continued his story: "The sheep left. When last seen they were using great energy in getting somewhere else." The officer repaired the lines without further interference.

Overall, Pershing's communications system proved to be reliable. France's Marshal Ferdinand Foch, Commander of the Allied Armies, went out of his way to use American telephones whenever possible, and Pershing used the telephone in his car to talk to officers at the fighting front.

The Signal Corps strung tens of thousands of miles of wire crisscrossing France during the Great War, or according to one writer: "enough wire to [circle] the earth four times at the equator." Remarkable for the time, all of Pershing's army was connected by telephone lines—from the port where the troops entered France to the soldiers in frontline trenches. World War I was the first time in the history of warfare when officers on the battlefield could have an instant telephone conversation with officers at headquarters. The telephone, telegraph, and radio connections supplied and maintained by the American linemen proved to be invaluable.

Soldiers in trench stay low while under attack. Courtesy National Archives.

After the war *Boston Globe* correspondent Sibley reported:

> *It would be unfair to close the record without speaking of the wonderful performances of the ... signalmen, who patiently ran wire through the shelled areas, going not in companies and with the help of close comradeship with their fellows, but alone through the dark, right out where the shells were dropping ahead of them, to the patient splicing of the wires broken by shellfire.*

The U.S. Signal Corps suffered 2,800 casualties in the Great War, second only to the U.S. Infantry, reflecting just how dangerous the telephone engineers' assignments were. Signal Corps personnel earned more than three hundred decorations.

General George Owen Squier, U.S. Army Chief Signal Officer, called the telephone system a monument to American genius. Historians agree that it was one of the most remarkable telephone and telegraph networks ever constructed for an army in the field.

General Pershing thought the communications system in France was one of the outstanding accomplishments of the war. His praised the Signal Corps, saying:

> *The officers and men and the young women of the Signal Corps have performed their duties with a large conception of the problem and with a devoted and patriotic spirit, as the perfection of our daily communications testify.*

Spotlighting Military Awards

MEDAL OF HONOR is the highest decoration awarded by the United States government. It's presented to members of the U.S. Armed Forces for conspicuous gallantry and valor, risking their own lives above and beyond the call of duty. The Medal of Honor is the oldest continuously issued combat decoration of the United States armed forces. It replaces the Badge of Military Merit established by George Washington to recognize "any singular meritorious action."

DISTINGUISHED SERVICE CROSS, the second-highest military decoration awarded to members of the U.S. Army and the U.S. Army Air Force, recognizes extraordinary heroism while engaged in action against an enemy of the United States. Actions must be more heroic than those required for all other combat decorations except the Medal of Honor.

DISTINGUISHED SERVICE MEDAL is the third-highest award to a member of the U.S. Armed Forces for exceptional or meritorious service during a war or in connection with military operations against an armed enemy of the U.S. Actions must be of a high merit but not meeting the requirements for the Distinguished Service Cross.

VICTORY MEDAL. This medal was awarded by the U.S. Army and Navy for military service in the armed forces from April 6, 1917 to November 11, 1918; or service in Russia from November 12, 1918 to August 5, 1919; or service in Siberia from November 23, 1918 to April 1, 1920. The Victory Medal signifies battle participation and campaign credit.

SILVER STAR OR CITATION STAR. The U.S. Army awarded this 3/16th-inch silver star for gallantry in action. It was placed on the Victory Medal ribbon. The award was established by Congress on July 9, 1918.

Images courtesy of Wikimedia Commons.

THREE
Hello Girls

"One night when Paris was under a rain of air bombs and when men rushed to safety ... the American telephone girls on duty were asked to leave their posts and seek ... shelter. Just then a window in the room was smashed by a shell fragment, yet those hello heroines remained at the switchboard. 'We will stay until the last man leaves,' they said. This is the fiber of the enlisted sisters of our fighting men."

—AMERICAN AUTHOR AND JOURNALIST ISSAC MARCOSSON

Here's how these plucky Hello Girls got to France.

General Pershing worked with French switchboard operators for a while but found they lacked skills in translating French into English and didn't understand the urgency attached to the job. He concluded that the American Expeditionary Force (AEF) needed trained, efficient U.S. switchboard operators who spoke French as fluently as they spoke English.

The Army advertised an "Emergency Appeal" in all major U.S. newspapers, calling for young single women to operate switchboards in Europe. The primary qualification was fluency in French and English. At a time when the public believed a

Poster shows a Hello Girl working at her switchboard while soldiers march past the window. Clarence Frederick Underwood, 1918. Courtesy Young Women's Christian Association via Library of Congress, Prints and Photographs, LC-USZC4-1421.

> *Mark Twain used the term "Hello Girls" to refer to telephone switchboard operators thirty years before World War I. In his book* A Connecticut Yankee in King Arthur's Court, *Twain wrote, "The humblest hello-girl along ten thousand miles of wire could teach gentleness, patience, modesty, manners, to the highest duchess in Arthur's land."*

woman's place was in the home, more than seven thousand young women volunteered to risk their lives working near the fighting front.

Two hundred and thirty-three women were selected from the flood of applicants. They were sworn into the U.S. Army Signal Corps and operated switchboards in seventy-five locations all over England and France. They were affectionately nicknamed the **"Hello Girls."** One proud Hello Girl spoke for many when she said that it was a privilege, not a duty, to serve her country, and she was inspired to do her utmost.

Thirty-three women were assigned to the first unit of operators sent to France.

One of them was Chief Operator Grace Banker, who recalled:

> *That first group of Signal Corp girls had come from all over the United States and from Canada. Some, like myself, were college girls; some came from public schools, and some from private schools. They all spoke French, but almost none had had any telephone experience until they were trained for the overseas service by the Telephone Company. Their ages ranged from 19 to 35.*

The army drilled the new arrivals in military discipline, just as they drilled male soldiers. They were subject to all army regulations. The army designed the operators' uniforms but required the women to pay for them. Each American female soldier arrived with a navy-blue uniform jacket and skirt, a white blouse, hat, overcoat, raincoat, black high-top shoes, brown army boots, and

The first Hello Girls arrive in France. Courtesy National Archives

black sateen bloomers—baggy undergarments that the young women called hideous but dutifully wore. The Signal Corps equipped them with helmets and gas masks. The operators lived in houses with a Young Women's Christian Association (YWCA) supervisor.

On arrival in France on March 23, 1918, Ms. Banker's unit was assigned to the Advance Section Headquarters in Chaumont, about 170 miles east of Paris in northeastern France. At the switchboard, the operators' overriding responsibility was to translate messages between the French and American officials. The women knew that one wrong word could have life-or-death consequences. Nineteen-year-old Louise Le Breton wrote home: "[We] worked ten hours a day. … It was tough going … It was drilled into us that every single call was so important."

Another young operator said that her job involved screaming her lungs out to soldiers in trenches over lines that were tied to trees and fenceposts or laid on the ground. Still, hearing an American woman's voice on the other end of the telephone line did boost morale among the AEF troops. One reporter wrote:

> *I reckon that the well-modulated, courteous and very American accents of a Hello Girl dripping in at the left ear have much the same effect on a homesick American as the soothing hand of a nurse on a sick soldier.*

After several months in Chaumont, General Pershing moved his headquarters north to Ligny-en-Barrois to be nearer the front line. Ms. Banker and five operators were assigned to Pershing's First Army Headquarters. There they would be connecting and translating thousands of vital messages.

The switchboard was installed in a house on the main street in Ligny. Sandbags were piled high around the outside for protection from bombs. The office was only a few miles from St. Mihiel, where over half a million American soldiers were ordered to assemble for battle.

Berthe Hunt said she and the other operators saw:

> *…the troops pass, the artillery rumble by, the trucks constantly going day and night. Supplies and men passed continuously until we thought all America had been sent over.*

The American girl soldiers handled an average of forty thousand words a day over the eight telephone lines leading out of the Ligny switchboard. Ms. Banker found the work fascinating but difficult, as much of it was in codes that changed frequently. Ester Fresnel agreed:

> *We were rushed to death; we worked day and night, six hours at a stretch,*

On the road to St. Mihiel. Courtesy National Archives.

and then ran home to snatch a few hours' sleep, then back to work. The strain was pretty bad. Everything came at once ... lines would go out of order, bombs or thunderstorms up the way. Still the communications had to go through. ... Altogether we were all very excited.

By mid-September an all-American army won its first victory of the war at St. Mihiel.

To keep up with the battle, Pershing ordered all of headquarters—including the telephone switchboards and the operators—packed up and rushed to Souilly, eleven miles southeast of Verdun and only a few miles from the Meuse-Argonne fighting zone on the Western Front.

The Meuse-Argonne offensive was the deadliest battle in American history at the time. On September 26, 1918, the Allied Armies launched a co-

Hello Girls manage the switchboards at St. Mihiel, helmets and gas masks hanging on the backs of their chairs. Courtesy National World War I Museum and Memorial.

ordinated series of attacks across the entire Western Front. More than one million U.S. troops joined the Allies' attack on the German Army. The goal was to reclaim territory that Germany had seized from France and Belgium. According to Bertha Hunt:

> *We were in an advance area, where we could see the red and yellow glare from the shelling and feel the [aftershocks] caused by the booming of the big guns.*

In Souilly the young women worked and lived in flimsy wooden sheds called barracks, surrounded by a sea of mud. Window frames were covered with oiled paper instead of glass. At night the windows were covered with black cloth to block any beam of light that might give away their location to German bombers.

Grace Banker recalled:

> *These funny old barracks proved to be fairly safe. While the [German planes flew] over us and bombed Bar-le-Duc and Ligny, we were spared.*

Thirteen telephone operators maintained twenty-four-hour switchboard service at Souilly, working from twelve to twenty hours a day. They worked tirelessly, as fast as they could, connecting headquarters to battlefields right to the edge of No Man's Land.

According to Hello Girl Hunt, one of the two switchboards "carried all the messages between the fighting units and the commanding officers directing their movements. Every order for an infantry advance, a barrage preparatory to the taking of a new objective and, in fact, for every troop movement, came over the 'fighting lines.' As we called them." She admitted that the responsibility for life or death messages made her "quite nervous."

During the most crucial battle on the Western Front, AEF Headquarters experienced a near catastrophe. A fierce fire started in one of the barracks at Souilly and destroyed eight buildings before being extinguished. The blaze threatened to demolish the switchboards and to disable the whole communications system, thus ruining the entire Argonne offensive.

When their barracks caught fire, the Hello Girls were ordered to leave. They firmly refused because calls were coming in from the front—and "every call involved soldiers' lives". They put their personal safety aside, defied

> *A bucket brigade is a line of people passing buckets of water from a water source to a fire. The person closest to the fire throws the water on the fire to extinguish it.*

authority, and ignored threats of Courts-Martial, to keep the communication system operational during the crucial battle. After the switchboards were secure, they willingly left the burning building. Chief Operator Banker remembered:

*The men and officers worked like mad [to put out the blaze], but a **bucket brigade** was powerless. Only the smoldering embers remained. Wires went down—the telephone line was out.*

Still, the plucky American women restarted service while the lines were being repaired.

For their courage and faithfulness to duty, the unit received this commendation:

> *This unit ... has performed invaluable service in handling the extremely heavy telephone traffic of Army Headquarters during two important operations of the war. The unit ... was burned out while stationed in Souilly. During this fire the only interest of the unit was to see that service was maintained and that ... the board and equipment was saved.*

After the war General Pershing praised the operators: "Their exceptional manner in discharging their duties, the fine *esprit de corps* (feeling of pride, fellowship, and common loyalty within the unit) and willingness to serve characterized the operating units in France."

Chief Operator Grace D. Banker received the United States Army Distinguished Service Medal for exceptionally meritorious and distinguished services. In addition, nineteen Hello Girls earned citations for excellent service.

All but one of the Hello Girls returned home after the war. The sad exception was Cora Bartlett, a victim of the influenza pandemic of 1918-1919, a global disaster that killed more than twenty million people.

Many of the Hello Girls took an oath to join the army; were outfitted, trained, and employed by the army; and thought they had enlisted in the U.S. Army. At the end of the war, however, they were dismissed as civilian employees of the army. Each of them was sent home without an honorable discharge and without veterans' benefits. The army denied that the women were enlisted because army regulations did not mention women. Only men were eligible to serve in the army in 1917—even though at the time, some twelve thousand female nurses served in the Army Nurse Corps. Sixty years passed before Congress granted the remaining Hello Girls veteran status and honorable discharges.

Signal Corps Hello Girls receive awards. Courtesy of Wikimedia Commons.

The fact that an estimated forty thousand women stepped up to help their country in various ways during the Great War helped the passage of the 19th Constitutional Amendment in 1920, granting women the right to vote in all states.

Years later Hello Girl Louise Barbour recalled that the year in France was crowded with interest, opportunities, and experiences that most of the Hello Girls still considered the "proudest and most important period of their lives."

Spotlighting the Switchboard

A 1917 switchboard desk consisted of rows of keys and plugs attached to cords. The back panel contained lamps (small lightbulbs) and sockets. When a customer called, a lamp lit on the back panel. The operator responded by plugging the rear cord into the socket next to that lamp. Then she flipped the front key forward and asked "Number, please?" The caller replied, and the operator then plugged the front cord into the socket for that number and flipped the front key backwards to ring the called party. The two telephone lines were connected, and the parties conversed. A lamp lit to alert the operator when both parties hung up. And then the operator pulled the plugs.

In 1917 every single telephone call was handled by the essential and efficient switchboard operator. At times the public expected more from the central operator than just putting through a call. One young operator reported being asked the price of carrots. Another caller wanted to know how to make oyster stew. In small towns, customers routinely called home simply by asking the operator to "Give me the house." These operators knew each of their customers by the sound of his or her voice.

Over time, technological advancements replaced manual switchboards and operators. Some customers, however, wished for a return to the days of the always-pleasant and helpful operator.

For more vintage telephone equipment, visit the New Hampshire Telephone Museum at 1 Depot Street, Warner, NH, or online at: www.nhtelephonemuseum.org.

Early telephone switchboard.
Courtesy New Hampshire Telephone Museum.

FOUR
Fighting 8th

"Fellows, you stand as pioneers on the frontier of your Race's progress. If you fail ... your Race's progress will be pushed back fifty years," Captain William Braddan, chaplain of the Fighting 8th Illinois National Guard Regiment, told his all-black troops before they entered the trenches in France. He also challenged them to erase "all doubts about your loyalty, discipline, and patriotism."

In 1917 many African-Americans shared the chaplain's hope that the Great War would offer black men a chance to prove themselves brave and patriotic soldiers.

The 8th Illinois National Guard Regiment consisted of African-American volunteers from the Bronzeville section of Chicago. It began as a militia in 1871. The regiment of four thousand men and forty two officers was unique because all the officers and men were African-Americans. It included some of Chicago's most respected black professionals. Its commander, Colonel Franklin Dennison, was a prominent attorney. Although they were a National Guard unit, the Fighting 8th had gained combat experience during the Mexican Border War in 1916.

The U.S. Army drafted 400,000 African-Amer-

True Sons of Freedom, **poster by Chas. Gustrine, 1918. African American Soldiers fight German soldiers in World War I, with a portrait of Abraham Lincoln above.** Courtesy Library of Congress, Photographs and Prints, 93503146.

51

ican men during the Great War. Only twenty thousand served in combat; the remaining 380,000 were assigned to manual labor jobs. The Fighting 8th was one of four African-American regiments that would fight in France during the Great War.

Before they sailed to France, the U.S. Army officially changed the 8th Regiment's name to the 370th Regiment of the 93d U.S. Infantry Division. The 370th debarked at Brest, France, in April 1918.

By the time the 370th arrived in France, the Allies had been fighting the Central Powers for four years, and the war in the trenches was at a standstill. Despite continuous shelling, neither side was able to gain ground. The French and British Armies were battle-weary and their supply of young men was nearly drained.

Chaplain Braddan, who traveled with the 370th throughout the war, recalled his first impression of the French people in his memoir, as follows:

The battered remains of Ypres, Belgium, during the Great War. Courtesy Heritage Image Partnership Ltd / Alamy Stock Photo.

France is truly bled white as far as her manpower goes. My heart ached as I watched the sad eyed women all in black mourning for loved ones killed by the [Germans].

Private John Lewis Barkley, a Missouri farm boy, wrote of his impressions of the refugees who he passed while his unit was marching to the front:

One old man was so feeble he had to be crowded into a cart that was already overflowing with furniture and bedding. A yoke of cattle was dragging the cart, and an old woman with a shawl over her head stumbled along beside it. She had one child by the hand and another clinging to her skirts. At the other side of the cart walked a pretty young woman with a tiny baby in her arms.

  Sometimes they [the refugees] passed quite close to us. But they hardly glanced up to look at us. Just watched the ground ahead of them to try to keep from stumbling. The worst thing about it to me was the queer sort of dead look on their faces. As if they couldn't see anything or feel anything anymore.

At Allied Headquarters, Marshal Ferdinand Foch hoped the fresh U.S. troops would fill gaps in their lines; General Pershing wanted the AEF soldiers to fight as one unit under his leadership. But with the attacking German Army marching toward Paris, Pershing quickly realized the situation was critical. If Germany captured Paris, France's troops and her people would be demoralized. The stakes were enormous; saving Paris would save France and perhaps the entire war. So Pershing agreed to "loan" the four black AEF regiments to the French. He'd been undecided about how to use his African-American infantry in the segregated U.S. Army. But the integrated French Army already had black combat soldiers from its African colonies fighting shoulder to shoulder with white Frenchmen.

A U.S. War Department survey of soldiers conducted at the end of the war revealed that many African-Americans found that the French people represented "the true democratic spirit, catering alike to all."

According to Robert Stevens, an African-American infantryman, "[The French] treated us with respect, not like the white American soldiers."

Another black soldier said, "France will always be looked upon by the American Negros as one shining example of democracy in this narrow world."

In contrast, white U.S. soldiers often found the French lacking the "modernism, cleanliness, and morals" of the United States. Many whites returned home with a firm belief that the U.S. was exceptional and superior to European countries.

Language was another problem for the Americans. One infantryman wrote to his aunt, "Take it from me it is a good thing for us that most of them know a little English or we would never get by."

When Pershing loaned the black regiments to the French Army, he assumed they would be used as laborers to free up French soldiers for fighting. But the French were sympathetic to the African-Americans' plight, as expressed by one French officer who said he did not "understand why Americans should treat one another so harshly and cruelly when it was momentarily expected that the division would be plunged into battle."

The French Army welcomed the men of the 370th Regiment as equals and used them to supplement their depleted and exhausted infantry. The fresh soldiers were outfitted with French machine guns, rifles, coats, and "funny little blue French helmets." They trained for six weeks in the town of Grandvillars in the Lorraine sector.

According to Braddan, they were housed with the "gentle folks of Lorraine who welcomed us into their homes and social life." He went on to describe Lorraine as one of the world's most beautiful places, "a garden spot." Based on the War Department's survey, in those homes where the American soldiers were respectful and helped with home and farm chores, they were

Soldiers of the 370th Infantry at Grandvillars in northeastern France where they train with the French Army. Courtesy Wikimedia Commons.

welcomed as family. But where they were brash and unruly, the French saw them as "ignorant of ordinary politeness, and wild."

Following their training under French officers, the regiment merged into the French Army. On July 24 they were ordered to the trenches at St. Mihiel to learn the strategy and technology of modern warfare and to experience life in the trenches.

The Germans feared African-Americans because they incorrectly believed that the "Black Devils"—as they called them—took no prisoners. Captured Allied soldiers reported that the first thing German interrogators wanted to know was how many "Black Devils" America had sent.

All summer long French officials moved the 370th from one hot spot to another along the Western Front. They traveled on foot and saw the chaos of war: streets and fields pitted with shell holes, entire towns in ruins, and hundreds of villagers fleeing behind the fighting lines with only a few necessary articles. They saw formerly quiet villages, beautiful churches, peaceful graveyards; now all a "heap of ruins."

Chaplain Braddan wrote home:

> *For days inhabitants have been evacuating village after village. I have seen caravans of women and children, old men and old women, trudging down long winding roads ... pulling improvised carts of all that is left of their earthly possessions. Homes ... left tearfully behind.*

In July, Colonel Franklin Dennison, commander of the 370th, was relieved of his command because of poor health. Colonel Thomas Roberts replaced him. A few days later the 370th saw action in the Argonne sector.

In a drive against the Germans, the Chicago regiment captured almost nineteen hundred prisoners, four cannons, forty-five trench mortars, and two hundred machine guns, inspiring Colonel Roberts to describe his new unit as "excellent material." Bold individual acts demonstrated the Americans' courage in battle.

- Lieutenant Harvey Taylor endured six wounds while leading a raid yet continued to lead his men.
- Private Spirley Irby, a runner who carried messages to and from head quarters under heavy enemy fire, was badly wounded and struggled to crawl and drag himself the last stretch to deliver a message.
- Private Arthur Johnson suffered a wound caused by a shell fragment

that lodged in his back. The private continued his duties until he came across a wounded buddy in No Man's Land. Ignoring flying bullets and his own pain, Johnson helped the barely conscious soldier almost a mile to the first aid station. Then he continued delivering ammunition.

- When a hand grenade landed among a group of soldiers in a trench, Corporal Isaac Valley tried to cover it with his foot in order to protect his men. He was severely wounded.

Chaplain Braddan wrote the following in a letter to his Chicago congregation on August 19, 1918:

> *It's a safe bet that when you receive this, we will be formed into a division and be used as shock troops, to lead the charge against the*

US African-American troops march northwest of Verdun, France, November 5, 1918. Courtesy Jonathan Mitchell/Alamy Stock Photo.

enemy and after drawing their fire, retire. This we will do for three or four days, then retire to the rear, rest for two days, replenish our regiment, and go at them again. When you hear that we are being thus used, don't protest; it's a glorious calling—and none but the brave fight like this. While it's the most dangerous, it's the most glorious. This is war, C'est la Guerre.

On September 16 the regiment pushed on to Mont-des-Signes, a heavily fortified city in the Soissons sector, about sixty miles east of Paris along the Western Front. They enjoyed the heartwarming cheers that greeted them as they marched through the French countryside. Villagers of all ages waved and shouted, "Vive les Américains! Vive la France! [Long live the Americans! Long live France!]"

Lieutenant Colonel Otis Duncan, one of the 370th Regiment's officers, described the action in the Soissons sector:

Beginning September 27, 1918, we sailed into [the Germans] and drove them back to the Aisne Canal, where they made a stand, facing us not 50 yards away. The fighting here was fierce. The Germans had placed barbed wire entanglements in the canal, but we avoided these with pontoon bridges [floating bridges] and continued our drive. We reached what was known as Mont des Signes, or 'Monkey Mountain.'

We took up our position here between 'Monkey Mountain' and the German line near a narrow-gauge railroad. Here we encountered more concrete emplacements [obstructions], dugouts, and barbed wire, and in getting to the Germans every man of us had to climb up on that railroad embankment, where we were fair marks for any kind of shell the German sent over. Naturally, we lost many of our men.

During the battle that raged from September 27 to October 4, the 370th faced continuous artillery shelling. The men responded heroically.

- Sergeant Matthew Jenkins led his platoon through an onslaught of fire to capture a fortified German tunnel by turning the enemy's guns on the Germans themselves. For thirty-six hours, the platoon held this position—without water or food—until reinforcements arrived.
- Private Charles T. Monroe took charge of his platoon when their commanding officer was killed. Monroe instructed the troops to continue firing even though the enemy was targeting them. The shelling was so intense that the Americans' trench guns were buried in dirt and debris. Monroe himself was buried by one nearby explosion. The men managed to dig him out; he continued to lead the charge.
- Zigzagging through machine-gun and sniper fire in No Man's Land, Sergeant Lester Fossie rescued a trapped and badly wounded messenger and helped him to company headquarters.
- On September 28 the 2nd Battalion of the 370th broke through German lines and destroyed multiple machine-gun nests.

The final offensive of the war involved all Allied Armies positioned along the Western Front. This, the largest offensive in history, began early in the morning on September 26, 1918.

Captain Ernest Piexotto, a combat artist during the Great War, witnessed the beginning of the massive offensive from an overlooking hillside near Montville in the Normandy region of northwestern France and nine miles north of Rouen. He recalled the experience in his memoir:

> *Just before three [AM] the air was split by violent concussions. A battery of 155s [155mm howitzer guns] in the very next room, so to speak, suddenly woke to action; some naval guns 'around the corner' rocked the ground with the force of an earthquake. The great barrage had begun.*

Never, we are told, in the history of the world, was such a barrage put over as on that morning. In the short American sector alone, four thousand guns were speaking, and the men were officially notified that this was no mere local offensive but one grand push from the North Sea to the Vosges [Mountains in Switzerland].

The French *Croix de Guerre* medal (French for cross of war) awarded for acts of heroism involving combat with the enemy. Courtesy Bjørn Christian Tørrissen, CCBY-SA3.0. via Wikimedia Commons.

On October 27, the French brigade that included the 370th, joined the offensive in the western section of the front line near the Franco-Belgian border. They were tasked with the job of pushing the enemy back into Belgium.

Braddan described the men of the 370th that day, saying:

… barefooted, ragged, and lousy [suffering with body lice]. Everyone was moon-eyed, haggard, unshaven, and half-crazed as a result of sleepless nights and anxious days.

In their pursuit under heavy enemy shelling, the African-American soldiers sometimes covered more than twenty miles in a day. They captured the Hirson-Meziéres Railroad, a significant supply line for the Germans, and Verte Place, Belgium, their main objective about seventy-nine miles south of Brussels. The 370th crossed into Belgium before news of the cease-fire reached them. And so, the nearby small village of Petite Chapelle has the distinction of being the only Belgian location that was liberated by African-Americans on November 11, 1918.

The 370th Regiment served with distinction in the Great War at St. Mihiel,

Argonne Forest, Mont des Signes, Oise-Aisne Canal, Soissons, Lorraine, and others. They served under French command and African-American officers during the entire war. Seventy-one men of the regiment earned French Croix de Guerre medals (French Cross of War), twenty-one were awarded U.S. Distinguished Service Crosses, and one soldier received a U.S. Distinguished Service Medal, making the regiment one of the most decorated units in the AEF.

The 370th suffered ninety-six deaths and 184 wounded. From their ranks of four thousand, almost 2.5 percent were killed. The average ratio for all AEF units was 1 percent. There can be no doubt that the African-Americans endured their share of blood and suffering.

Victory Monument, **located at 35th Street and Martin Luther King, Jr. Drive in Chicago, honors the African-American soldiers of the 370th Regiment who fought in the Great War. Leonard Crunelle designed the monument. Its three panels depict an African-American soldier, an African-American woman, and the figure of Columbia holding a tablet listing the regiment's major battles. The monument was dedicated on November 11, 1928. Photograph by Joe Ravi, CCBY-SA3.0.** Courtesy Wikimedia Commons.

Irving S. Cobb, a U.S. journalist with The Saturday Evening Post, wrote that victory in the Great War will not be "an all-white victory by any manner of means." General Pershing praised the African-American soldiers saying:

> *I cannot commend too highly the spirit shown among the colored combat troops, who exhibit a fine capacity for quick training and eagerness for the most dangerous work.*

As the 370th prepared to leave France, French General Joseph Vincendon, commander of the French 59th Division, praised the regiment in a General Order to all the soldiers:

> *You [the 370th Regiment] have given us your best and you have given it out of the fullness of your hearts. The blood of your comrades who fell on the soil of France, mixed with the blood of our soldiers, renders indissoluble the bonds of affection that unite us. We have, besides, the pride of having worked together at a magnificent task, and the pride of bearing on our foreheads the ray of a common grandeur. A last time—Au revoir [French for goodbye].*

Spotlighting Regimental Bands

During the patriotic swoosh of men joining the Great War, professional African-American musicians signed up to travel with black regimental bands in France. Led by African-American bandmasters, they brought blues and jazz to Europe.

George Edmund Dulf, a Chicago musician, conducted the band of the 8th Illinois National Guard. When the Great War erupted, he moved into the regular army's 370th Regiment, along with all the other soldiers of the Fighting 8th. Dulf, a veteran of black minstrel shows, had been associated with the Fighting 8th since 1898. Under his direction the Regimental Band of thirty musicians played classical, popular, blues, and jazz.

The 370th Regimental band became known for being in the thick of battle. At Metz near St. Mihiel, the band marched alongside the attacking 370th combat troops—the only military band to do so. They played "Illinois," the official state song, while marching into the "very teeth of German guns." On another occasion the band was performing in a quiet sector when an unexpected dogfight between French and German airplanes exploded overhead and pelted shrapnel down on the band and the audience.

The most popular song during the Great War was a catchy number called "Over There." Its patriotic lyrics and upbeat melody inspired the troops in Europe as well as folks at home. The hit song ends with a rousing "And we won't come back till it's over, over there."

The original sheet music and lyrics can be explored at the Library of Congress website: https://www.loc.gov/item/ihas.100010517/. To listen to an authentic recording of "Over There," visit the National Jukebox: https://www.loc.gov/audio/?q=over+there.

Over There. **Sheet music cover, 1917.** Courtesy Library of Congress.

Our Regular Divisions. Recruiting poster by James Montgomery Flagg, 1918. Courtesy Library of Congress, Prints and Photographs, LC_USZC4-10225.

FIVE
Code Talkers

"… I was born here in America and being a Real American I will fight and die for it," Francis Nelson, a Native American Sioux Indian, wrote to Newton D. Baker, Secretary of War, dated February 10, 1918.

Native Americans have a centuries-old tradition of defending their land and people. This warrior creed of defending the land may have been the primary reason many Native Americans volunteered to fight during the Great War.

When the U.S. joined the European war, the "first Americans" enlisted even though they were not obligated to serve. At the time, many of them had not been granted the right to become U.S. citizens, did not have the right to vote, and were not required to enlist. Nevertheless, over seventeen thousand registered for military service and about ten thousand Native Americans joined the American Expeditionary Force (AEF) in Europe. The AEF ranks included members of the Choctaw tribe, primarily a farming tribe from Oklahoma, who were assigned to the U.S. 142nd Infantry, 36th Division.

The 142nd Infantry arrived in France in July 1918. Their first assignment was in the Argonne Forest along the Western Front, where some of the heaviest and most prolonged fighting of the war occurred.

One U.S. artillery private described his first impression of the Argonne battlefield as cold, muddy, and rainy with thousands of crushed-down trees and shells bursting everywhere. He admitted that the amount shelling "had every man of us scared."

In September, the battle in the Argonne Forest was not going well for the Allies. German intelligence repeatedly tapped into the Allies' telephone lines, picked up Allied radio signals, and captured far too many human messengers. German code-breakers were skilled and quickly cracked the Allies' codes, which were based on mathematical progressions or European languages. Consequently every troop movement and battlefield strategy was anticipated and blocked by the enemy. The Germans knew where Allied forces were headed and where the Allies' supplies were kept. They were always prepared and one step ahead of the Allies.

Tapping into telephone lines was routine during the Great War. The most common way to tap a telephone wire was to run a wire parallel to the source wire. The tap wire acted as an antenna and picked up magnetic leakage from the source wire. The tap picked up the spoken message and transmitted it to the enemy.

Frank Sibley, a corresponding reporter for the Boston Globe, recalled:

> *The need for care in telephoning was impressed on us ... The assumption was that the Germans listened in on our lines by using induction lines alongside. The new order said, 'It is safe to assume that all telephone conversations within a thousand yards of the front line will be heard by the enemy.'*

Colonel A. W. Bloor, commander of the 142nd infantry, observed: "There was every reason to believe every … message going over our wires also went to the enemy. … We felt sure the enemy knew too much."

During the forty-seven-day Meuse-Argonne campaign, Colonel Bloor heard a few of his Choctaw soldiers speaking their native language. Bloor and the Choctaws agreed that the Army should try using the Choctaw language to send and receive messages. As infantrymen they had experienced first-hand the desperate need for secure messages on the battlefield. Considering that few Native American languages had ever been written down, the Germans were extremely unlikely to be familiar with their language. Bloor decided to test the theory.

The plan to use "code talkers" was tried during a movement of several American combat units on October 26, 1918. Choctaw Code Talker Solomon Bond Louis was stationed at Division Headquarters, and Choctaw Code Talker James Edwards was on the other end of the telephone line. Edwards, in an actual combat zone and speaking in the Choctaw language, told Louis significant battle information. At headquarters, Louis translated the message into English for the commanding officer. The commander's response was translated back into Choctaw and telephoned back to Edwards at the front line.

As there were no Choctaw words for some military terms, the code talkers used a combination of Choctaw words. For example, the Choctaw words for "big gun" were substituted for artillery; Choctaw for "little gun shoot fast" indicated a machine gun; "arrows" meant ammunition; and "stones" referred to grenades. The code talkers had created a code within the code.

Following the test Colonel Bloor reported, "The enemy's complete surprise is evidence that they could not decipher the messages."

Nineteen Native American Choctaws, the original code talkers, sent and received coded telephone messages in their native language for the remainder of the war. Historians say that the Choctaw code talkers made a significant contribution to the success of the Meuse-Argonne battle and speeded up the end of the war. Years later a former German officer admitted that German intelligence was "completely confused by the Indian language and gained no benefit whatever from their wiretaps."

One Choctaw code talker, Private Joseph Oklahombi, is among the most famous Native American heroes of the Great War. In October 1918, Oklahombi and about twenty buddies got cut off from their unit, Company D, 141st Infantry, 36th Division.

Private Oklahombi earned two medals for daring action in the St. Etienne sector of France, about two-hundred-fifty miles southeast of Paris. U.S. General John Pershing presented Private Oklahombi with a Silver Star for bravery. French General Henri-Philippe Pétain awarded Oklahombi a *Croix de Guerre* with the following citation:

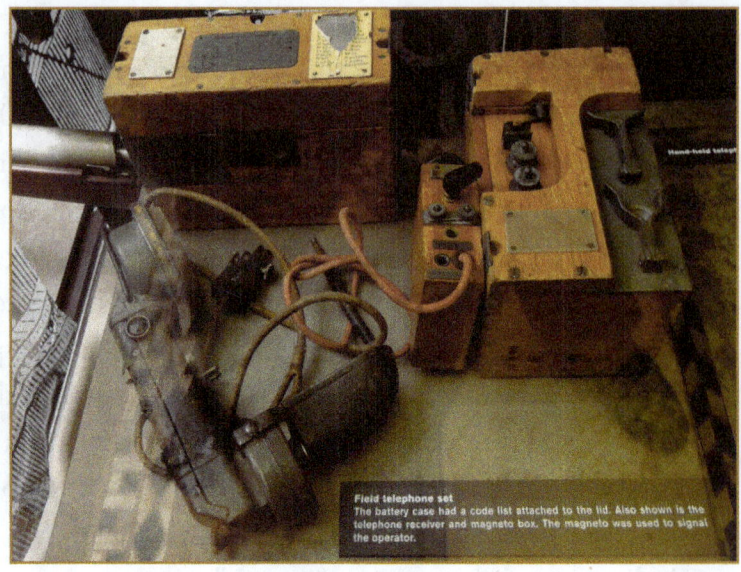

Great War Field Telephone equipment includes a receiver (bottom left) wooden battery case (top left) and magneto box (right). The hand-cranked magneto, a generator that uses magnets to produce electric current, was used to signal the operator. Courtesy Daderot Photography/National World War I Museum and Memorial Exhibit/Wikimedia Commons.

> *Under a violent barrage, [Pvt. Oklahombi] dashed to the attack of an enemy position, covering about 210 yards through barbed-wire entanglements. He rushed on machine-gun nests, capturing 171 prisoners.... and a number of trench mortars. Turned the captured guns on the enemy, and held the position for four days, in spite of a constant barrage of large projectiles and of gas shells. Crossed no man's land many times to get information concerning the enemy and to assist his wounded comrades.*

Of the ten thousand Native Americans who fought in the Great War, about five hundred Native Americans, 5 percent, were killed in action. This ratio may reflect that Native Americans were frequently assigned to the more dangerous duties, such as messengers, scouts, and snipers, possibly because of skills attributed to American Indians in early Western fiction.

During the battle at the Argonne Forest, one 142rd Native American expressed his pride and grit after he was wounded twice and gassed: "I felt no American could be or should be better than the first Americans, therefore, I did not linger in the hospital."

During the Meuse-Argonne offensive, one officer observed that Native American troops were always in the front line and if one went down another stepped up to fill the gap.

Marshal Ferdinand Foch, Allied Supreme Commander, said that he would never forget the "brilliant service of the valorous Indian soldiers," and their energy and courage.

These Choctaw soldiers pioneered using Native American languages as military codes. Their success shortened the war and saved thousands of American and Allied lives. They also paved the way for the future use of Native Americans as code talkers.

General Pershing praised the Native Americans' contributions to the war, saying:

U.S. soldiers use an abandoned German field telephone near St. Mihiel in northeastern France during the Great War. Courtesy Alamy.com

Choctaw Code Talkers' Congressional Medal of Honor, presented in the U.S. Capitol Building on November 20, 2013, recognizes the original Code Talkers for their dedication and valor during the Great War. The medal depicts a soldier on his field phone writing "Tamampo chito," Choctaw for "big gun." Courtesy U.S. Mint via Wikimedia Commons.

The North American Indian took his place beside every other American in offering his life in the great cause where, as a splendid soldier, he fought with the courage and valor of his ancestors.

Native Americans were granted citizenship through the Indian Citizenship Act of 1924. Historians agree that their wartime service was the primary factor for granting Native Americans citizenship. The Act of 1924 also gave Native Americans the right to vote; however, state regulations for voting rights varied. In some states Native Americans waited thirty more years for the right to vote.

Official national recognition of the Choctaw code talkers was delayed because the knowledge that Native American Indian languages were being used to transmit coded messages was necessarily kept top secret for decades.

President George W. Bush signed into law the Code Talkers Recognition Act on November 15, 2008. The law read, "The service of Native American code talkers to the United States deserves immediate recognition for dedication and valor" and honors every Native American code talker who served in the U.S. military during either World War One or World War Two. The Choctaw tribe was awarded a Congressional Gold Medal. Each code talker received a duplicate silver medal, along with a commendation for "serving proudly with honor and distinction."

Spotlighting Native American Art

For centuries, Native Americans have recorded tribal and personal events by painting descriptive scenes on buffalo hides. Around 1860, however, the great herds of buffalo and other game were dwindling, and the tribes were adjusting to living on reservations. With fewer buffalo hides, artists turned to painting on used ledgers, leather bound accounting books that merchants and traders had discarded.

Artists painted directly on top of the numbers on the ledger pages. New drawing tools—colored pencils, crayons, ink pens, and watercolor paints—became available to the artists as well. Native American Ledger Art brought a new, finely detailed look to the traditional drawings that illustrate oral storytelling and record important events. Over time Native American artwork transformed from military conquests to scenes of ceremony and daily life.

Today Native American Ledger Art is gaining attention. Museums are exhibiting original ledger drawings. Current Native American artists are creating new work in the style of "old ledger art."

You can read the Choctaw legend of the Wind Horse at the First People website: www.FirstPeople.us/FP-Html-Legends/TheTaleoftheWindHorse-Choctaw.html.

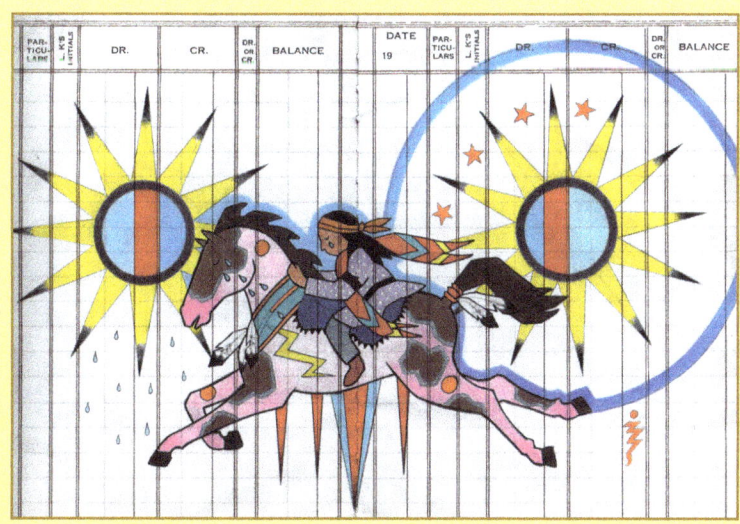

"Choctaw Legend of Wind Horse" created in the style of "Old Ledger Art" by Choctaw Native American, Karen Clarkson.

SIX
Carrier Pigeons

"There has long been a controversy among pigeon breeders as to whether it is instinct, intelligence, or abnormally keen sight which enables a [carrier] pigeon to find its way back from points many hundreds of miles away. Perhaps a combination of all three must be admitted," E. I. Farrington wrote in the August 1918 issue of The New Country Life.

Carrier pigeons are trained to return home and conditioned to deliver messages while wearing a leg canister or a backpack with straps tucked under their wings.

Reports of pigeons delivering messages go back centuries, as far back as ancient Egypt. Throughout the 1800s, France and England had official pigeon postal services. The pigeons even delivered mail between London and Paris, a flight of 212 miles. The birds delivered information faster than any other delivery service before telegraphs and telephones became available.

European military officials, noting the success of the pigeon postal service, created pigeon units in their armies. Belgium, France, England, and Germany raised and trained thousands of carrier pigeons before war erupted in 1914.

Feral Racing Pigeon in Flight. Photograph, Richard Bedford. Courtesy Alamy, Inc.

Carrier pigeons, unsung heroes of the Great War, became a vital link between the battlefield and headquarters. The birds have a unique homing instinct that scientists still do not completely understand. They can fly a mile a minute, cover long distances, and reach high altitudes. They are intelligent, brave, persistent, and reliable. They eat very little. And they can find their way home even through the thick smoke of military guns. Enemies found it hard to stop the small, swift, smart, tough messengers.

During the Great War carrier pigeons lived in mobile lofts mounted on wagons or trucks. Each loft was a cage with wire or wood-spindle sides that

A carrier pigeon mobile loft is mounted on a British truck used in France during the Great War. The unique paint on the truck helps the birds find their loft even if the truck has been moved. Courtesy Photo Researchers, Inc., Photographer/Science History Images/Alamy, Inc..

housed twenty birds comfortably. The loft's roof was painted several bright colors that the birds could identify easily from the air. When pigeons were needed on the battlefield, they were taken from their loft and transported to the front in wicker baskets worn like backpacks.

Soldiers wrote critical messages in code and packed them into a canister attached to the carrier pigeon's leg. The pigeon handler launched the messenger from the battlefield. With keen eyesight and instinctive homing skills, they would find their way back to the loft, even if the mobile loft had been moved. The bird's return would trigger a bell that alerted the handler to retrieve the message. Carrier pigeons delivered messages to raise an alarm, relay locations, report progress, and convey other key information.

Carrier pigeons were particularly valuable when the infantrymen fought outside the range of their telephone network or when the telephone wires got blown up. The birds even served on ships, submarines, and aircraft. It was risky and dangerous for both the pigeons and their handlers. More than 100,000 carrier pigeons served in the Great War. They successfully delivered 95 percent of their messages. The birds are credited with saving thousands of lives as well as changing the course of battles.

General Pershing saw the value of the European birds and created a Pigeon Service within the U.S. Signal Corps. At full strength the Signal Corps Pigeon Service consisted of nine officers, 324 soldiers, six thousand pigeons, and fifty mobile lofts.

One U.S. carrier pigeon named Cher Ami (French for dear friend) became a famous hero. His bravery shone while traveling with the 77th Division of the American Expeditionary Force (AEF) during the Argonne offensive.

On September 26, 1918, the first day of the Argonne offensive, Private John Nell's unit, the 2nd Battalion, 77th Division, was ordered to go "over the top."

The command to "go over the top" ordered the infantry to climb out of the trenches and begin an attack through No Man's Land.

CARRIER PIGEONS

The unit was surrounded by a dense fog so thick that the men couldn't even see each other. Nell described the battlefield as completely covered with tangled barbed wire, old shell holes, dead trees, brush, and logs, with a thick underbrush of briars and vines that were nearly a solid wall. He wrote in his memoir:

> *It was terrible. I stumbled, fell down, and when I tried to get up, I was all tangled up in barbwire and briars. I tried to pull and tear loose; but the more I tried to get loose, the more I would get tangled. The barbwire was thick and as high as my head. I finally got loose and started on.*
>
> *The Germans' shells were coming thick and fast. We could see the flash from the German guns on a far-off hilltop. We had not gone far until our own artillery began firing [over our heads], and the shells kept getting thicker and thicker. ... The roar of the guns and the shells bursting both in front and behind us was a terrible feeling. ... It seemed like the whole earth was trembling. I was dizzy and my ears were ringing, and I was almost crazy from fear.*

Nell and others from his unit got separated from the division and ended up inside German territory. More than six hundred U.S. soldiers regrouped in a valley called "the pocket."

The unit realized that they were in an indefensible position, surrounded by heavily armed German troops who were on higher ground. The Germans knew where the Americans were and the Americans knew they were trapped.

Nell wrote the following in his autobiography:

> *There are no words to depict the terrible conditions and the terrible emotions we encountered during the next five days and nights,*

> *[October 3 through 7, 1918]. Imagine nearly 600 men thinly concealed on the bottom edge of a steep hillside. … We were huddled tightly together, a complete violation of everything learned in training. Yet our group was so pinned down by machine gun, rifle, and mortar fire that we could not spread out further and gain better cover.*

That night the men in the pocket dug out shell holes, pits for one or two men, to use as shelter from bombardments. Shell holes provided a slightly safer place below ground level. Infantrymen retreated into shell holes when they were in open fields where there were no trenches. Private Nell recalled:

> *I was still carrying an old broken hoe I had picked up. We [Nell and one buddy] would break the dirt and rocks loose with the hoe, then dig it out with our hands. At about the time we were dug in, we were told to eat. That order, under other circumstances, might have seemed funny. Many of us had no rations whatsoever. After we finished our*

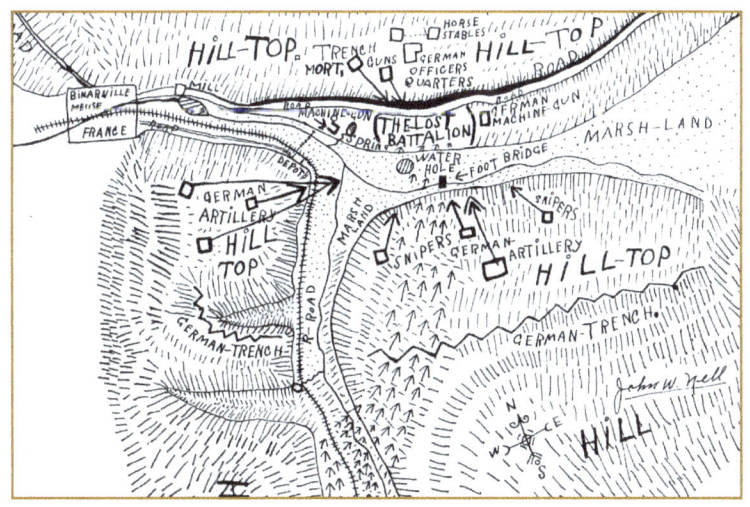

This hand-drawn map was sketched by Private John Nell. It depicts significant points inside and surrounding the "Pocket" where the Lost Battalion was trapped during the Meuse-Argonne offensive. Courtesy: John W. Nell, *The Lost Battalion, A Private's Story*. Historical Publishing Network, San Antonio, TX, 2001.

> Reinforcements in this military context refers to assistance in the form of additional ground troops and aircraft equipped with guns and bombs.

meal, or our wished-for meal, and got our holes dug, … we settled down for the night.

The next morning only about two hundred men in the pocket were well enough to fight. They had no food or medical supplies. Nell said that food didn't matter much to him; the shelling and machine-gun fire kept him "under such constant strain and fear that food was not a priority." All he could think of was to be on guard at all times and do what he could to survive.

Scouts went out with desperate messages asking for **reinforcements.** They either were blocked and returned or were never heard from again.

Because human runners couldn't break through the German line, Major Charles Whittlesey, Division Commander, released several carrier pigeons to alert Allied Headquarters of their location, the dangerous trap, and the need for reinforcements. Headquarters dispatched help, but a powerful German army stood between the reinforcements and the trapped men.

Just when it seemed their situation couldn't possibly get any worse, it did. Nell relates:

> *A barrage came plowing its way down the hill directly toward us. It blew dirt high in the air as it moved on across the valley. There was absolutely nothing we could do. We had to just take what came, knowing without a doubt that it was our own artillery. It stopped right on our position and continued well over an hour. It just seemed like it was going to get all who were left alive.*

Major Whittlesey whipped out his notebook and hastily jotted down this plea:

We are along the road parallel 276.4. Our own artillery is dropping a barrage directly on us. For Heaven's sake, stop it.

Whittlesey
Major 308

The major handed the message to Private Omar Richards, the unit's pigeon handler. With artillery shells crashing all around them, Richards nervously inserted the message into a canister. He reached into the wicker cage and grabbed one of the two remaining pigeons. Just then a shell exploded

U.S. Army Signal Corps messenger pigeon with handler, 1918. Courtesy National Archives.

near him and startled Richards. The bird, equally startled, slipped from his hands and flew off.

Everyone stared at the fleeing bird. Richards apologized repeatedly and reached for Cher Ami—the unit's last pigeon. The black-and-gray-checkered bird was an experienced messenger who had successfully delivered messages throughout the war. The bird knew well the route to headquarters. Private Richards clipped the canister to Cher Ami's leg. Private Nell wrote:

> *We knew without a doubt that this was our last chance. If that one lonely, scared pigeon failed to find its loft, our fate was sealed. We would go just like the others.*
>
> *When [Richards] let this last pigeon loose, it flew up and landed in a tree near my position. We all started throwing rocks and sticks at the bird so it would continue on its way and not be a target for the German snipers.*

Richards shook the tree; the worried bird watched. With artillery shells falling all around him, Richards climbed the tree and shook the branch where Cher Ami was sitting. Much to the unit's relief, Cher Ami took off in the direction of headquarters.

Cher Ami escaped through the heavy enemy fire, but he reached his home seriously injured. He'd been wounded in the chest, one eye was missing, and one leg was gone. Miraculously he still bore the canister with the critical message. The injured bird had bravely persevered in spite of his deep wounds and the horrific, exploding battlefield.

Army medics valiantly worked to save the courageous bird.

Meanwhile at headquarters, troops from the 305th, 306th, 307th, and 308th U.S. Divisions, as well as French soldiers and tanks were dispatched to battle the German stronghold surrounding the pocket. Allied forces fought through cannon fire, bombing attacks, and machine-gun blasts.

On October 8, the outnumbered and outfought German Army retreated. Private Nell said that he could hardly believe it was over. He wrote the following:

> *It was like being reborn. My thoughts then went to our dead and wounded. What a shame and pity it was that so many had to go as they had. So many were wounded and still in terrible pain. I knew many of the men would never survive with their wounds. It was not long until the incoming boys were sharing what little rations they had with us. It felt like we had been saved from death, hanging on by our last string of hope.*

Gun crew firing machine guns at the enemy's entrenched position. Courtesy National Archives.

There were only 194 men left out of nearly 600 men. We were a dirty, muddy, ragged outfit. Some of the boys' clothing was in shreds, with no leggings and the knees worn out. The clothing had been torn and ripped to pieces crawling through the masses of tangled barbwire and brush from the very beginning of the advance.

The unit became known as the "Lost Battalion," even though headquarters had always known where the trapped soldiers were. The problem was getting through the enemy stronghold.

At headquarters, the brave little pigeon recovered and retired to a quiet life in the United States. Cher Ami earned a Croix de Guerre (French Cross of War medal) from the French Government for valor and a Citation from the U.S. Army for heroic service.

Major Whittlesey earned a Medal of Honor, the highest U.S. military award. Twenty men of the Lost Battalion received Distinguished Service Crosses for gallantry.

Cher Ami. Courtesy Smithsonian Institution.

General Pershing praised Major Whittlesey as one of three outstanding heroes of the war and considered the men and events in the pocket one of the greatest stories of courage and determination in the AEF. Major Whittlesey gave credit to the troops who freed the men in the pocket, saying, "The real story is with the men who, day and night, fought for our relief."

Near the end of Private Nell's autobiography, he challenged the sincerity of government officials when they said that soldiers "died gloriously for their country." Nell wrote, "The ones I saw died pitifully, just doing their duty."

Today Cher Ami is included in an exhibition titled "The Price of Freedom: Americans at War," at the National Museum of American History. For more about Cher Ami and the Lost Battalion, visit: https://www.si.edu/Encyclopedia_SI/nmah/cherami.htm.

Spotlighting Rags

In 1918 a homeless mixed-breed terrier with a fluffy tail roamed the streets of Paris, France, searching for food, shelter, and friendship. Sergeant James Donovan, a Signal Corps specialist with the 7th Field Artillery, and Sergeant George Hickman, 16th Infantry, stumbled upon the abandoned terrier and took him to Donovan's camp with the 1st Division AEF. Donovan repaired breaks in the telephone lines on the battlefield—usually while battles raged overhead. He named the terrier Rags because his shaggy fur made him look like a bundle of rags.

While with the 1st Division, Rags located injured soldiers and summoned help. The brave pup raced through barbed wire and gunfire delivering messages. His quick thinking and speed saved many lives. Rags accompanied the Sergeant when he repaired telephone lines on the battlefields, running ahead to spot breaks in the lines. With his excep-

Rags and his friend, First Sergeant George Hickman, 1925.
Courtesy Wikipedia.org.

tional hearing and keen sense of smell, Rags warned the soldiers of incoming shells and alerted them to the first sniff of gas. Although he didn't like it, he dutifully wore his gas mask. The plucky 1st Division mascot became a hero.

During the brutal Meuse-Argonne offensive in October 1918, both Donovan and Rags were wounded and gassed while repairing lines. Rags had shrapnel wounds and lost sight in one eye. The sergeant suffered multiple wounds and severe gas poisoning. They were rescued and taken to a field hospital where medics allowed Rags to sleep under Donovan's bed. The terrier was soon back on his feet, but Sergeant Donovan's injuries were more serious— so serious that he was sent home to be treated in the hospital at Fort Sheridan near Chicago. Rags went along. Sadly, James Donovan's lungs failed. He died at Fort Sheridan. Rags grieved for his best friend.

By 1920, however, the mascot-hero had become a permanent member of a Fort Sheridan family with two young girls. The girls cared for and loved Rags for the rest of his life.

To read more about Rags, look for the book, From Stray Dog to World War I Hero: The Paris Terrier Who Joined the First Division, *by Grant Hayter-Menzies, University of Nebraska Press, 2015.*

SEVEN
Combat Artists

"The war artist puts on a steel helmet, his gas mask, his trench boots, his trench coat and laden with only a sketch book, a couple of pencils and some emergency rations in his pockets, like any soldier present, he takes his chances." George Matthews Harding, an Official Combat Artist, described how he began his day in 1918.

Combat Artists during the Great War were uniformed soldiers commissioned by the government to create an eyewitness pictorial record of war.

Artists have recorded the history of wars in paintings and sketches for centuries. John Trumbull, an artist who painted scenes of the American Revolution, is generally recognized as America's first Official Combat Artist. Trumbull enlisted as a private in the army during the Revolution. General Washington noticed Trumbull's sketches and requested that the artist serve as his aide-de-camp, commissioned to sketch battlefield plans and layouts.

When the U.S. entered the Great War, records of the war were already being created. Illustrators designed posters to recruit enlistees. Cartoonists

Valley of the Marne at Mont St. Père, George Matthews Harding, 1918, charcoal, pastel, crayon. **Aerial perspective of the shell-torn town clogged with troops, horses, and equipment. A British airplane and an observation balloon fly above.** Courtesy Smithsonian Institution.

drew political cartoons to shape public opinion. Photographers captured pictures showing the stark reality of war. Newspaper journalists described events for their readers. Nevertheless the U.S. War Department wanted an artistic pictorial record of the war as well.

The army selected eight experienced artists to serve as Official Combat Artists of the American Expeditionary Force (AEF), dubbed the "Army Eight." They were commissioned as captains and were recruited to create an accurate record of the war in sketches and paintings. Chaumont, 170 miles east of Paris near the Western Front, served as their base. All were professional artists, primarily illustrators for magazines and books. The Army Eight were free to go wherever they wished as long as AEF Headquarters knew where they were. These uniformed army captains—armed with pencils, pens, and paintbrushes—walked onto the battlefields of France and used their talents to record history.

This was the first time the U.S. Army commissioned artists to serve as eyewitnesses on the battlefields and make pictorial records of the war. It was dangerous, as Captain Townsend recounted: "I had just gotten well into a drawing when I was startled by a tremendous explosion near me. ... Pieces of rock, and, as I imagined, shell [pieces of a bomb] were falling all around me, as well as dust from the ruined masonry."

Despite dire conditions, these combat artists created hundreds of dramatic images of the war.

Combat artist George Matthews Harding worked as an architect by day and studied art at night in Philadelphia. Later he became an art professor at the University of Pennsylvania. While working for *Harper's Monthly Magazine,* he traveled around the world—a trip that shaped much of his artwork. Captain Harding was the only AEF artist to use a camera for gathering material that he later sketched. The Pennsylvania artist's routine was to make as many as sixty sketches, notes, and photos on location, and later in his studio turn them into complete pictures. He wrote in his diary that, in addition to

Crossing the Pontoon Bridge, Château Thierry, **William James Aylward, 1918, crayon, gouache.** Courtesy Smithsonian Institution.

dodging enemy fire, the combat artist also faces "the usual problems of one's craft, to be solved perhaps in a cold drenching rain, with a sketch book held under one's trench coat making each pencil mark mean something."

William James Aylward's sketches often include waterfronts, harbors, and ships. The Milwaukee-born artist explained his interest in nautical scenes: "As my father was a ship builder ... and vessel owner in a small way, sailing his own schooner on the Great Lakes, I naturally inclined toward 'sea-stuff.'" Aylward studied at the Art Institute of Chicago and the Art Students League in New York City. He worked as a magazine illustrator. Captain Aylward worked in watercolor, pastel, and oil paints. His paintings of seaports and docks are among the most beautiful of the AEF collection.

Like Aylward, Walter Jack Duncan also studied at New York's Art Students League and worked as an illustrator. Nicknamed the "wizard of pen

Newly Arrived Troops Debarking at Brest, France, **Walter Jack Duncan, 1917, ink wash.** Courtesy Smithsonian Institution.

and ink," he once marveled that a pen-and-ink illustration "sparkles enchantingly against its sunny background of white paper." During the war Captain Duncan documented vital activities behind the front lines. He spent time with the Supply Department and created permanent records of the artillery school, debarkation centers, salvage shops, and gun shops. Many of his wartime sketches reflect his interest in architecture and landscapes. In "Newly Arriving Troops Debarking," Duncan's skill as an illustrator shines.

Unlike most of the artists who grew up near cities, Harvey Thomas Dunn was born into a homesteading family in the Dakota Territory. His father farmed. Dunn began sketching on the blackboard in the one-room rural schoolhouse that he attended. Later he illustrated novels and magazines. He said that he wanted his war sketches and paintings to show "the character of the struggle and the men engaged." To create his sketches Captain Dunn used a large portable sketch box with rollers on two sides. The rollers held a continuous scroll of drawing paper. When he finished a sketch, he simply turned the rollers so that the image curled up inside the box and a clean section of sketch paper unrolled, ready for the next sketch. Dunn chose to march with the troops during battles in order to lend realism to his battle scenes. His combat art is the most popular of the AEF collection.

Wallace Morgan aspired to a career similar to his father's career as a painter and an art instructor in Albany, New York. Morgan studied art at the National Academy of Design. He refined his skills while working as a newspaper artist. At the time, newspapers depended on artists to do what photographers do today. Morgan said that the experience taught him to put "life

On the Wire (in No Man's Land), Harvey Thomas Dunn, 1918, **pastel, charcoal.** Courtesy Smithsonian Institution

Infantry and Tanks Advancing on the Field, **Wallace Morgan, 1918, charcoal.** Courtesy Smithsonian Institution.

and action" into his illustrations. It proved to be excellent training for a future combat artist. Many of his sketches depict the landscapes of war. Morgan followed the marines to St. Mihiel and the Argonne Forest to capture action on the battlefields. His technique was to make quick pencil sketches and notes in small sketchbooks. Later, in his studio, he translated the rough sketches into finished drawings. He preferred to use brushes, even for line drawings.

Forty-nine-year-old Ernest Clifford Peixotto was the oldest combat artist. He studied art at San Francisco's Mark Hopkins Institute and later in Paris. He spoke fluent French and knew his way around France. He often served as a translator and guide for the other AEF artists, especially his "three comrades," Captains Duncan, Morgan, and Smith. Peixotto traveled with the troops. At times he was under fire. Once he survived an enemy night raid. The artist described conditions during the Argonne offensive as "Rain and slush; mud and dirt; my paper wet and soggy, my hands numb with cold." He added that these were not the best conditions for sketching.

Jules Andre Smith awed critics with his huge body of work in multiple media. He was born in Hong Kong, China, into a sea captain's family. Later the family settled in New York City. Smith studied architecture at Cornell University but chose to work as an artist. When America entered the war, Smith enlisted and worked in a camouflage unit. His talents were quickly recognized, and he was selected for the Army Eight. Smith worked rapidly and produced detailed, accurate work. He was the only combat artist who had been trained to be a soldier, so he was appointed senior officer of the group. Captain Smith arranged exhibits of AEF art at headquarters in Chaumont for the officers to view the artwork before it was shipped to Washington,

Bombarded Town in the North, Toul Sector, **Ernest Clifford Peixotto, 1918, charcoal.** Courtesy Smithsonian Institution.

At Romorantin Airfield in France, **Jules Andre Smith, 1918, charcoal.** Courtesy Smithsonian Institution.

D.C. He defined all the AEF artists' work as truthful and honest depictions of military life "without resorting to sensational tricks and fakes."

When the U.S. joined the war, Harry Everett Townsend was creating war posters. He was born in the small town of Wyoming, Illinois, into a merchant and farming family. He painted signs for local businesses while he was a high school student and later studied at Chicago's Art Institute. Townsend financed his art education by servicing farm implements. His work appeared in Harper's and other magazines as well as in books. Townsend's specialty was illustrating war machinery, guns, and tanks. He also sketched aircraft and aerial scenes, which may have been in memory of his brother, who died while serving with the British Royal Flying Corps.

After the war ended, Captain Peixotto sketched the Allied Armies of Occupation crossing the Rhine River, the Franco-German border at Coblenz. He described the event at Coblenz in his memoir, as follows:

Just before dawn [December 13, 1918], I heard a sound I had been listening for; the sound of shuffling feet on the wooden Bridge of Boats below my window, and looking out, could see in the first dim light of day a long yellowish serpent crawling slowly across the bridge. ... Tramp, tramp, tramp, went its thousands of marching feet—but no other sound broke the stillness of that early morning.

Toward nine o'clock I saw the first American flag go over. ... The morning was gray and misty with a drizzling rain. Then, against all this monotony of tone, there appeared a radiant object—a brilliant spot of red, white, and blue, edged with its golden fringes—the silken

A Forced Landing Near Neufchâteau, **Harry Everett Townsend, 1918, charcoal.** Courtesy Smithsonian Institution/National Museum of American History.

regimental colors of the infantry, "Old Glory" triumphant, carrying its message of humanity and justice to the peoples beyond the Rhine.

Some of the Army Eight's work was published immediately in American newspapers and magazines. Other pieces appeared in exhibitions. The AEF Official Art is a permanent visual record of America's contribution to the Great War. More than five hundred works of AEF Official Art are archived at the Smithsonian Museum. Over the last hundred years, art critics have praised the collection as exceptional examples of combat art.

See more of the AEF Combat Art Collection at the Smithsonian's National Air and Space Museum, Independence Avenue at 6th St. SW, Washington D.C. Images of the artwork can also be viewed online at https://www.si.edu/spotlight/wwi100.

Spotlighting Floating Bridges

A bridge of boats, also called a floating bridge or a pontoon bridge, is a bridge that floats on water, supported by floats called pontoons. Empty barrels, timber rafts, inflated rubber floats, flat-bottomed boats, even small barges have been used as pontoons. To build a floating bridge, soldiers linked the pontoons together and anchored them to the shore. Then they constructed the surface of the bridge from a series of wood planks, placed crosswise on top of the pontoons. Side rails held the planks in place.

Each pontoon can support a load equal to the mass of the water that it displaces. If the maximum load of a bridge section is exceeded, one or more pontoons may become submerged and sink. A pontoon bridge could also sink if one section is weighted down more heavily than the other sections. Because floating bridges block river traffic, most are constructed only for temporary use during wartime or in emergencies.

Earlier in this chapter William Aylward's Crossing the Pontoon Bridge shows a temporary pontoon bridge supported by boats.

American soldiers construct a pontoon bridge over the Marne River at Château Thierry, France, September 1918. Courtesy National Archives.

EIGHT
Flying Schoolgirls

"The pilot sat out in front (and not strapped in!) with nothing but air between him and the earth," according to one 1912 airplane pilot. "If anything went wrong, as it often did, the aviator was the casualty."

The Wright brothers changed the world forever with their successful test flight at Kitty Hawk, North Carolina in 1903. Orville and Wilbur Wright, engineering geniuses, designed and built a biplane that Orville flew to achieve the world's first controlled flight.

By 1910, ten years before Amelia Earhart's first flying lesson, a few rare women and men had embraced the thrill of flying in the open sky. Early pilots looked for ways to earn money while flying. Many turned to flight exhibitions—shows where pilots demonstrated their skills by flying loops or figure eights, sky writing, and more. Flying demonstrations, and a chance to go up in an airplane, attracted and enthralled audiences across America.

The first open-cockpit biplanes were "no frills"

U.S. Air Service recruiting poster showing a large barrage balloon, dirigible airships, and biplanes surrounding the red, white, and blue U.S. Air Service insignia, 1917. Lithograph print, Forbes Publishing. Courtesy Alamy Inc.

machines. They lacked seatbelts, radios, windshields, heat, lights, parachutes, and steering wheels—pilots controlled the plane with levers and switches. Navigation systems for early pilots were paper maps strapped to their thighs. Early flying was hazardous, and stunts like wing-walking were insanely risky.

Harriet Quimby, the first American woman to earn a pilot's license, had a fatal accident just eleven months after she was licensed. Unfortunately, the two-seater airplane that Harriet was flying, for unknown reasons, pitched too far forward. Both Harriet and her passenger were flipped out of their seats and fell to the ground. Seatbelts soon became required equipment.

Meanwhile, more cautious pilots chose to deliver airmail for the U.S. Postal Service. Airmail pilots flew in open cockpits through all kinds of weather. To protect themselves from rain, snow, and icy wind, they wore fur-lined leather flying suits, boots, helmets, and even face masks.

When the United States joined the Great War, a few brave women aviators were eager to do their part by piloting airplanes in France. Even though women did not yet have the right to vote and everyone believed that a woman's place was in the home, these young women pilots were determined to fly with the U.S. Army. But when each woman applied, the War Department responded that the army did not accept women—although at the time some twelve thousand female nurses served in the U.S. Army Nurse Corps and at least one hundred telephone operators had been sworn into service with the U. S. Army Signal Corps. Nevertheless, the patriotic aviators shelved their dreams of military flying and searched for other ways to serve their country during the war.

Katherine (Katie) Stinson was twenty-one years old when she earned her flying license in 1912. Only three other women in the entire country were licensed pilots at the time.

Katie participated in flight exhibitions around the country, performing aerial stunts, precision landings, and night-flying with flares. She was one of the first women to execute a vertical loop, called "looping the loop." Just

Katherine Stinson and her modified Curtiss JN-4 "Jenny" biplane. Courtesy Bain News Service via Wikimedia Commons.

five feet tall and weighing a mere one hundred pounds, Katie became America's darling. Newspapers referred to her as the "Flying Schoolgirl" because reporters were convinced she was only sixteen. The Flying Schoolgirl flew record-breaking trips. The most notable was her flight from Chicago to New York City, with stop-overs. That trip established an American endurance record.

When the U.S. entered the Great War, Katherine applied to the War Department to be a military pilot. She was turned down with a polite "Women need not apply." So she volunteered to help the American Red Cross raise money for wounded soldiers through flying exhibitions and fundraising tours. While flying over towns and cities, she dropped leaflets urging the "folks down there on earth" to contribute to the Red Cross.

Ambulances on the way to the hospital. Courtesy National Archives.

But Katie wanted to be involved in the action in Europe. The Flying Schoolgirl signed up to drive Red Cross ambulances across the battlefields of France. It was hard, stressful, and life-threatening. At the end of the war Katherine was worn out and ill. Back home, she was diagnosed with tuberculosis. Katie recovered, but she was not strong enough to continue flying; sadly, that career ended. Katie was one of the few early flyers who could have resumed flying after war if her health had allowed.

Based on her experience, Katherine Stinson believed, "If you are going to let other people decide what you are able to do, I don't think you will ever do much of anything." She also advised young women that "There is nothing about flying that makes it unsuited to a woman. It doesn't demand size or strength."

Another young woman, twenty-two-year-old Bernetta Miller from Canton, Ohio, caught the flying bug. Bernetta learned to fly at Moisant Aviation School in Mineola, New York.

One month after she received her license, she was off to College Park, Maryland, to demonstrate the capabilities of the Moisant Company's new monoplane—an airplane with one wing instead of the two stacked wings of a biplane. The U.S. Army Signal Corps was interested in the Moisant-Blèroit airplane for military use. Bernetta was chosen to demonstrate the plane for the army. She believed that the only reason she was chosen for the test flight was because she was a woman. She said that the army would naturally assume that if a woman could fly the plane, "so surely could a man."

In spite of her success and natural ability, Bernetta gave up flying after a few years. She believed it lacked career opportunities and was simply too

Blèroit XI monoplane, the type of airplane Bernetta flew. Courtesy Wikimedia Commons.

expensive. And with war raging, she wanted to do her part. Knowing the army would not accept women, even women pilots, she joined the Women's Overseas Service League and went to France.

Bernetta worked in a canteen near the battlefields at St. Mihiel and later Argonne. The ex-pilot provided hot chocolate (popular with troops), coffee, food, medical supplies, and other necessities for the soldiers. The fighting was intense. Because so many soldiers were wounded, canteen workers were asked to help in the field hospital. They frequently worked under enemy fire, and Bernetta was wounded.

Bernetta received the French Croix de Guerre and a U.S. citation lauding her "devotion to duty, disregard of personal danger, and untiring energy." She said of her experience at the frontlines:

War zone canteen, Bernetta Miller on the right. Courtesy National Archives.

> *I wouldn't say I had a rough time at the front because it was the men who had a rough time. There were men who had been lying in the field for several days. The division asked us if we would help. One memory I shall never forget. Anything we did for a man under those circumstances—and many of them probably died within 24 hours—he invariably said, 'thank you' or 'God bless you.'*

Two months after Bernetta passed her flying tests, a twenty-one-year-old woman, Ruth Law, received hers. Ruth began flying at Burgess Aviation School in Marblehead, Massachusetts. When Ruth received her pilot's license in November 1912, she was one of six women pilots in the country. In an interview with a Christian Science Monitor reporter, Ruth explained her love of flying:

> *There is an indescribable feeling which one experiences in flying; it comes with no other sport or navigation. It takes courage and daring; and one must be self-possessed, for there are moments when one's wits are tested to the full. Yet there is an exhilaration that compensates for all one's efforts.*
>
> *I shall never forget my first flight. I had the sensation of being shot out of a gun, as we rose from the earth. Then, slowly, I grew used to the feeling, and the joy of rising up into the air and watching the earth recede took possession of me. There is a great sense of the noise of the machine at first, but soon even that seems to fall off behind. The wind against the face is splendid, and to watch the villages, towns and cities, just pretty patches on the earth, from that nearness to the fleecy clouds, gives a spice to the sport that I find in nothing else."*

Pilot Law's greatest achievement was setting an American long-distance record when she flew nonstop from Chicago, Illinois, to Hornell, New York.

Ruth Law in her Curtiss Pusher biplane modified with Wright levers and switches. Courtesy Wikimedia Commons

Ruth flew her Curtiss Pusher biplane that everyone was sure was too small and outdated for such a long flight. Many felt a woman would not have the endurance—could not stand the numbing cold and would become too fatigued—to fly such a long distance. Ruth had her own reasons for attempting this flight. She hoped to set a nonstop flight record and she wanted to prove that women are competent aviators. Against all odds the determined pilot completed the flight and set a new American record for distance of a nonstop flight. Ruth Law became a star, a celebrity, and a legend. The press crowned her "Queen of the Air."

During the Great War, Ruth was determined to be a military pilot. She went straight to the White House to visit President Wilson and request permission to join the AEF Aviation Unit in Europe. The president refused, saying that women were not permitted in the army. The disappointed pilot was inspired to write an article titled "Let Women Fly!" for Air Travel magazine. In the article, she argued that a woman's success in aviation should prove a woman's fitness to work in aviation.

Somehow Ruth did manage to get permission to wear an official army uniform for exhibition flights and leaflet "bombing" flights—flying low over towns and dropping leaflets (paper bombs) that encouraged Americans to buy Liberty Bonds. The pilot was well-liked, and the public responded.

After the war Ruth continued aerobatic flying until 1922, when the Queen of the Air retired at her husband's request.

Two other women pilots—Marjorie Stinson, Katherine Stinson's younger sister, and Helen Harris—chose to teach flight lessons rather than perform stunts. Marjorie soloed and earned her pilot's license on August 12, 1914. At eighteen years old, she was the youngest licensed pilot in the country.

Marjorie taught flight lessons at the Stinson family's flight school in San Antonio, Texas.

With the Great War roaring through Europe, the Royal Canadian Flying Corps sent their cadets to the Stinson School of Flying for training. Marjorie trained about eighty Canadian cadets. She also trained Texas civilians for service in the American Flying Corps. Marjorie's students nicknamed her "The Flying Schoolmarm." The young schoolmarm often reminded her students that up

Liberty Bonds were a method for the U.S. Government to raise money to help pay war expenses. By buying a bond, Americans were loaning money to the government. The government promised to repay the money plus interest on a specified date.

Front and back of circular advertisement depicting a smoking bomb. Ruth "bombed" neighborhoods with these leaflets to encourage the purchase of Liberty Bonds. Courtesy Smithsonian Institution/National Air and Space Museum.

Historic Curtiss JN-4 "Jenny" biplane, photograph by Kletr. JN-4 biplanes were built by Curtiss Aeroplane Company in Hammondsport, New York, beginning in 1915. They were widely used by the U.S. Army and Navy to train cadets. With two seats and dual controls, the student was able to sit in front of the instructor. After the Great War Jenny biplanes were used to delivered U.S. air mail. They were also preferred for the stunt flying and aerobatic displays at flight exhibitions. Courtesy Shutterstock.com.

in the air in a small plane is no place to settle a "difference of opinion about how to fly."

Marjorie also flew to raise money for war-related causes. Near the end of the war, the U.S. Government took over the job of training military pilots, ending Marjorie's schoolmarm career.

Helen Hodge Harris, an Omaha, Nebraska native, learned to fly at the Christofferson School in San Francisco, California. The twenty-three-year-old soloed and received her license on November 12, 1916.

One of her trainers advised her to "line up with the safe and sane element" of the aviation business for the good of everyone in it. Helen followed this advice and flew her Curtiss biplane mainly for pleasure.

During the war Helen trained pilots for the U.S. Aviation Cadet Pilot Training Program, created by the U.S. Army Signal Corps. On graduation from flight school, the pilots became officers in the Signal Corps or in the Signal Officer Reserve Corps.

Helen believed that "Nothing is impossible."

These inspiring women pilots took giant steps to challenge the existing limits of what women are able to do.

Spotlighting The Red Cross

When the U.S. joined the Great War, the American Red Cross's mission was to offer humanitarian aid to American and Allied soldiers as well as civilian victims of war, with special attention to the children of Europe.

Before the U.S. joined the war, as part of a preparedness program the American Red Cross agreed to assist the Army by readying complete hospital units for transfer to the government in an emergency. Many civilian hospitals around the nation organized such units. During the war the units were shipped to France, where they staffed primary treatment centers for wounded soldiers. These doctors, nurses, and ambulance drivers worked under difficult conditions for long hours. They treated infected wounds, mustard gas burns, trauma, and more.

The American Red Cross also operated canteens in France to serve all Allied soldiers. Red Cross volunteers, mostly women, transported supplies to hospitals, camps, and canteens through the American Red Cross Motor Corps.

At home, the Junior Red Cross, middle-graders through college students, knitted scarves for soldiers, rolled bandages, and built furniture for hospitals. They sewed garments and collected relief supplies for European refugees. Younger members filled Friendship Boxes with school supplies and personal items for children in Europe. They packed Christmas boxes with toys, books, dominoes, and things they made, like ragdolls and mittens. Many members also cultivated War Gardens.

Today, American Red Cross volunteers and employees continue to provide safe, reliable blood services through voluntary donations, and compassionate care for servicemen, their families, and disaster victims.

Have YOU a Red Cross Service Flag? Jessie Willcox Smith, 1918. Young boy posts a Red Cross Service Flag in the window below a Christmas wreath. Service Flags were displayed as part of a nationwide Christmas Eve candle-lighting ceremony honoring all U.S. troops serving in the war. Courtesy American Red Cross and Library of Congress Prints and Photographs LC-USZC4-3188 via Dover Publications, Inc.

His Bunkie, William James Aylward, 1918, watercolor. Courtesy Smithsonian Institution.

NINE
Peace

"Peace! It was too good to be true."

—Private John Barkley.

The Meuse-Argonne Offensive was the largest and bloodiest operation of the Great War for the AEF (American Expeditionary Force). Allied forces attacked the German Army along the entire Western Front for forty-eight days, beginning September 26 and ending November 11, 1918. The Allies persevered and recaptured much of the territory Germany had seized earlier in the war.

In October of 1918 the Central Powers began to crumble:
- Germany was on the brink of civil war. Citizens had lost confidence in their ruler, Kaiser Wilhelm II, and they wanted to be free of his rule.
- Bulgaria signed a cease-fire agreement with the Allies on September 29, 1918. Austria-Hungary requested a cease-fire in late October. The Ottoman Empire collapsed and signed a cease-fire agreement on October 30. By November, Germany was the only Central Power still fighting the war.
- The German Army was exhausted and their numbers were dwindling. Germany no longer had fresh troops to replace its losses, while the supply of Allied troops seemed endless. One German

> *An armistice is a formal agreement among warring countries to stop fighting and to negotiate a lasting peace. An armistice is a cease-fire agreement. It is not a surrender and does not always end the war.*

general reported morale was so low that his troops surrendered in hordes when attacked.

- German generals told Kaiser Wilhelm that there was no hope of winning the war. German soldiers had no interest in going on; the government was weakened; the people were starving and rebelling. The generals recommended that Germany plead for an **armistice** before Allied forces invaded Germany.

In November Kaiser Wilhelm stepped down, fled to the neutral Netherlands, and never returned to his home country. With no other options, Germany was forced to ask for an armistice.

A German delegation met with Marshal Ferdinand Foch, commander-in-chief of the Allied Armies, on November 7 to discuss the terms of the armistice agreement. The terms required that Germany evacuate all occupied territories in France and Belgium and surrender all lands it had seized in Europe since 1914. Germany would turn over its military weapons, ships, and submarines to the Allies. Furthermore, Germany would be required to pay billions in gold marks to compensate for the destruction of the war. The agreement also stipulated that German ports would continue to be blockaded until the peace treaty was signed.

The German delegation found the terms too harsh and filed a formal protest. But there was no question of negotiation. With their army depleted and exhausted, the German delegation was in no position to refuse to sign. They signed the armistice agreement at 5:00 AM on November 11, 1918. Promptly, Field Orders from Allied Headquarters announced, "Hostilities will cease upon the entire front at 11:00 o'clock, 11 November 18 French time."

"Calamity Jane's" gun crew fired the last shot of the war for the Allies near Meuse, France, 1918. Courtesy National Archives.

Reporter Frank Sibley submitted the following account from the frontline:

The artillery kept it up till the last minute. But there seemed to be little hate in that morning's barrage. The [Allies'] guns weren't pointed anywhere in particular; just in the general direction of Germany and turned loose as fast as they could be fired.

As the hour approached, officers and men of the artillery gathered at the batteries, all eager to fire 'the last shot in the war.' At one battery, a long rope was fastened to the lanyards of each of four guns. About two hundred men got their hands on the ropes. One man with a watch [stood by]. On the hour, he dropped a handkerchief.

A thousand men sagged back on the firing ropes; four guns barked simultaneously, and a thousand Americans let out a yell that must have been heard in [Germany].

Another American correspondent reported that he had never experienced anything quite like the electrical jolt he felt when the guns suddenly stopped at 11 AM. He said that the roar stopped like a motor car hitting a wall and the quiet was eerie.

Private John Barkley was recovering from wounds in a small French town when he heard a "wild commotion." The townspeople were running through the streets yelling "Vive la France!" A soldier passing by told him that the armistice was signed. Barkley recalled:

Celebration in Alsace-Lorraine sector of France. Courtesy National Archives.

> *We went back to our old quarters that night. But we didn't do much sleeping. We'd got so cannons didn't bother us, but we weren't used to the kind of noise that went on in that French town, all night long. There were mobs in the streets. ... They danced and sang. They sent up rockets and flares and laughed and shouted and cried. ... Peace! It was too good to be true.*

When she learned of the armistice, Hello Girl Merle Egan said she and two friends wanted to "celebrate in some small way, so we wandered down to the main square where the celebration was in full swing. The French had gone mad and the French soldiers were more amorous than usual. They felt, since America had saved them, Americans must be kissed."

Correspondent Frank Sibley described his view that evening:

> *As the darkness grew thicker, the hoarded fireworks, the flares, and rockets, ... began to soar up into the night. From Division Headquarters, we could see the glow in the sky as far away as the Argonne Forest, and of course all around our own front. For miles the heavens were reddened and dotted and scored by the flaming show. It beat any Fourth of July I ever had seen, for besides our own somewhat scanty supply there were the boundless stores and the crazy enthusiasm of the French soldiers.*

"At 4:30 PM every church bell in France began to ring," switchboard operator Cordelia Dupuis wrote in her diary. "The French people were screaming in the streets. All the engineers got together and paraded with tin pans and sticks ... making all the noise they could."

An American visiting Paris exclaimed: "A frenzy of joy sweeps over the civilized world. Victory! Peace!"

Although the fighting stopped with the armistice, Allied statesmen took

Signing the Peace Treaty in the Hall of Mirrors, William Orpan, 1919. The Treaty of Versailles was signed in the Hall of Mirrors within the historic Palace of Versailles, twenty-minutes from Paris, France. Heads of many nations attended the signing, including U.S. President Woodrow Wilson, seated fifth from the left. German officials signed the treaty on June 28, 1919, agreeing to officially end the Great War. Courtesy Wikimedia Commons.

six months to negotiate the terms of the peace treaty. France wanted very strict restraints on Germany so they would never again threaten to ignite a war in Europe. The British Prime Minister argued for more lenient terms so Germans would not build up resentment. The U.S. President Woodrow Wilson proposed forming a League of Nations to settle international disagreements peacefully. In the end most of France's tough terms were written into the treaty.

No German leaders were invited to the treaty negotiations. When they were given an opportunity to review the treaty, they interpreted it to single out Germany as the only country responsible for starting the war. This stipulation riled Germans for years. They believed other countries' actions forced them into the war. Once again they objected, but could see no alternative to signing the treaty. They were in no position to renew fighting. At the Paris Peace Conference—held in the Hall of Mirrors within the Palace of Versailles—Germany and the Allied countries signed the Treaty of Versailles on June 28, 1919, finally ending the war.

The Great War changed the world dramatically. It led to the formation of the first international organization charged with preserving peace throughout the world. The treaty established President Wilson's concept of a League of Nations to settle international disputes, later replaced by the United Nations, which is now more than seventy years old. The Great War helped the United States emerge as a world power. When it entered the war, the U.S. Army was the weakest among all major nations. The U.S. finished the war as the richest and strongest country in the world. And the fact that so many women assumed active roles in the Great War contributed to women gaining voting rights in the U.S. and other countries.

The peace treaty carved the European continent into many new, smaller countries and created new borders for existing countries. Germany, Russia, Austria-Hungary, and the Ottoman Empire lost territory. New countries formed or gained independence as a result of the war, including Czechoslovakia, Estonia, Finland, Latvia, Lithuania, Poland, and Yugoslavia.

Four empires that had ruled for centuries, sometimes harshly, collapsed as a result of the Great War and were replaced by new countries:

- The German Empire reorganized as the Weimar Republic. Parts of Germany were allocated to Denmark, Czechoslovakia, Belgium, France, and Poland.
- The Austria-Hungary Empire split into two separate countries, Austria and Hungary, and forced the ruling Habsburg family into exile. Portions of the empire's territory were annexed to Czechoslovakia, Poland, Yugoslavia, Romania, and Italy.

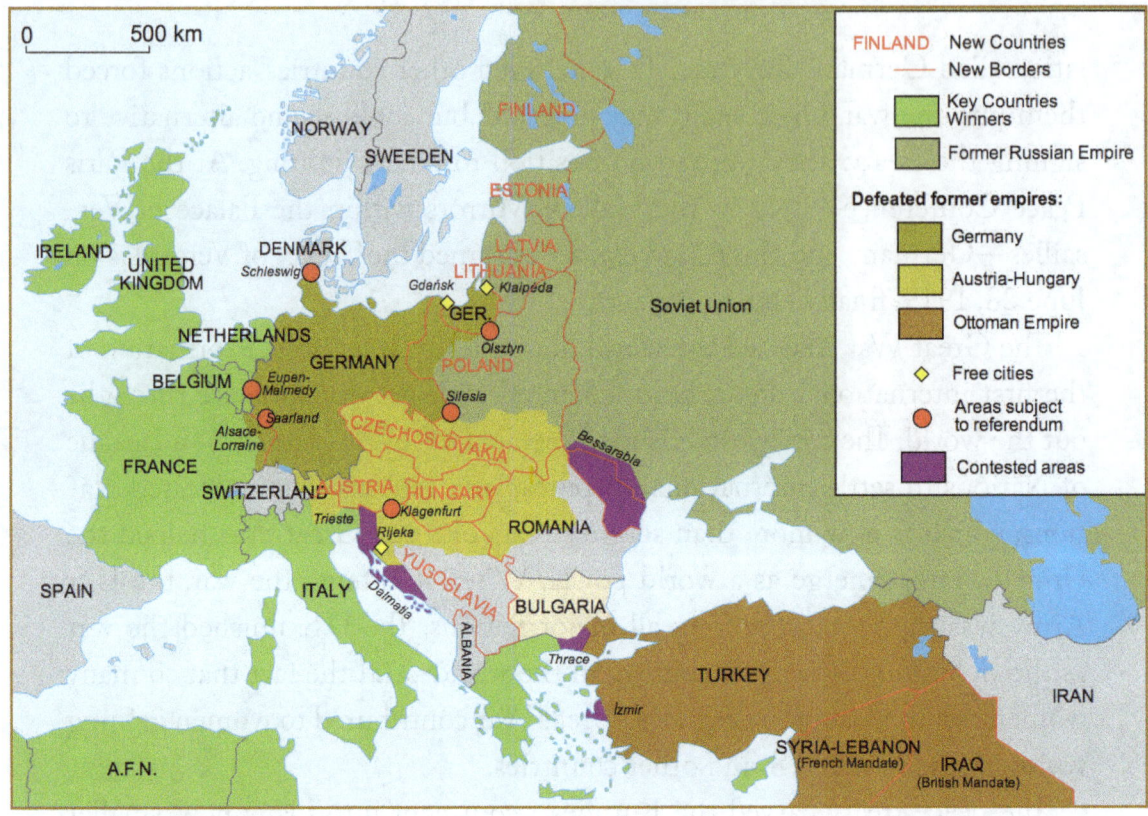

Map of Europe before the Great War with overlaid lines defining the new borders that were established by the Treaty of Versailles. Courtesy Wikimedia Commons, (Derivative work by Fluteflute Map Europe_1923-fr.svg: Historicair, CC BY-SA 2.5-2.0-1.0).

- The Ottoman Empire collapsed and surrendered after British troops captured Baghdad and Palestine. It became Turkey. Sections of the former empire were assigned to Saudi Arabia and Yemen.
- The Russia Empire was enveloped in a civil war that forced the ruling tsar to step down. The country's new government signed a cease-fire with Germany on March 3, 1918 and withdrew from the war. Russia's border territories of Estonia, Finland, Latvia, and Lithuania gained independence.

Military combat changed completely. The war began with a 19th-century military plan of hand-to-hand combat on open battlefields. It ended four years later with devastating 20th-century weapons of mass destruction. War became more violent and impersonal.

The Great War caused more deaths and human suffering than any previous war. In Europe it wiped out a whole generation of men—young men with dreams they would never have a chance to explore. An estimated sixty-five million men from around the globe were mobilized to fight in the Great War. Eight-and-a-half million were killed, twenty-one million were wounded, and eight million went missing or were taken prisoner. The war scarred those who survived. Ten million civilians died because of starvation, diseases, and accidents during the war. Cities and towns turned into burned and cratered rubble. Combining the costs of all combatant nations, the Great War cost an estimated $186 billion dollars, ($186,000,000,000.00) in 1914-1918 U.S. dollars.

Later many reflected on the war itself and grieved. Captain Robert Graves, a wounded British officer, penned in his autobiography:

> *The news [of the armistice] sent me out walking alone along the dyke above the marshes of Rhuddlan [an ancient battlefield in Wales, part of the United Kingdom of Great Britain] cursing and sobbing and thinking of the dead.*

Chaplain Braddon wrote:

> *How inconsistent that my government sent these willing subjects [African-Americans] to Europe to fight ... for democracy, while it denied the same to its most loyal and patriotic subjects, the Negros.*

Ernest Hemingway, an American journalist and author, said that the Great War was the most "colossal, murderous, mismanaged butchery" that has every taken place on earth. Hemingway was severely wounded by shrapnel while driving an American Red Cross ambulance in the war.

Private Nell, who survived five days and nights in the pocket, wrote this request:

> *The very thought of engaging in another war should be bitterly criticized and discouraged by all. But if there are no other ways and means to prevent it, and if we are invaded, then war it will have to be. But at least let us teach our young men there is no glory for the ones who make the supreme sacrifice and the ones who are disabled and carry the scars of battle.*

Despite the brutality of the Great War, when Americans were called to defend their country—the place they called home—they responded with inspirational bravery and patriotism.

After the war, General Pershing praised the spirit of the AEF troops in his final report to the Secretary of War:

> *The memory of the unflinching fortitude and heroism of the soldiers of the line fills me with greatest admiration. To them I again pay the supreme tribute. Their devotion, their valor and their sacrifices live forever in the hearts of their grateful countrymen.*

No doubt Pershing, if asked, would also have lauded the contributions of the many unsung heroes of the Great War, among them the civilians, volunteers, and even animals whose stories will hopefully never be lost, but instead will continue to inspire us as we strive for peace in our own time.

Spotlighting The Medal Ceremony

John Lewis Barkley is among the most decorated U.S. soldiers of the Great War. He earned a World War I Victory Medal with one silver and one bronze service star, a French Médalillemilitaire, a French Croix de Guerre with bronze palm, an Italian Croce al Merito di Guerra, a Medal for Military Bravery from the Kingdom of Montenegro and a U.S. Army Citation.

Young John grew up on a Missouri farm near Kansas City, Missouri, where he enjoyed fishing, hunting, and tracking. He was a skilled outdoorsman which served him well in the army.

Barkley joined the U.S. Army in 1917. The army trained Private First Class (Pfc) Barkley in the skills of a sniper, observer, and scout. He arrived in France in spring, 1918, and was assigned to an intelligence unit with U.S. Army Company K, 4th Infantry Regiment, 3rd Division where his duties included scouting enemy movements.

According to his U.S. Army Citation, Pfc Barkley was stationed at an observation post near the German frontline at Cunel in northeastern France on October 7, 1918. He was ahead of the Allied forces. Barkley, on his own initiative, repaired a captured enemy machinegun and mounted it in a disabled French tank near his post.

John Lewis Barkley, American Hero. Courtesy National World War I Museum and Memorial, Catalogue #1996.19.138.

He then singlehandedly broke up two enemy counterattacks, thereby saving Allies' lives and enabling Allied forces to gain and hold Hill 25.

By spring 1919, the fighting had stopped but many U.S. troops were still in Europe. Barkley's division, and other divisions, were ordered to assemble with a "bunch of generals" and military bands for a medal ceremony on March 17.

Private Barkley recalled:

All of a sudden, I heard my name called. ... The captain told me to get out there in front. I started out toward the officer who was reading the list of names. ... I was standing at the very best attention I could, but I was getting more nervous every minute. Then [General Pershing] was standing in front of me. He saluted, and I almost snapped my right arm off in answering. But I did it automatically. My head had about quit functioning. He stepped up close to me, did something with the front of my blouse [shirt]. He shook hands with me, congratulated me, and said something about a 'fellow Missourian.'... Then he sidestepped to the right and began decorating the next fellow. I heard one [General say to] his aide: 'He's just a kid!'

I still didn't know what it was General Pershing had pinned on me, so as soon as I dared I squinted down along my nose. I couldn't see anything but a little blue ribbon with white stars. But that was enough. I knew that the medal beneath it was the Congressional Medal of Honor!

Explore

TIMELINE OF EVENTS
1917

JANUARY Germany declares unrestricted submarine warfare

FEBRUARY U.S. learns of German telegram urging Mexico to invade U.S.

JANUARY Marjorie Stinson trains Royal Canadian Flying Corps cadets in Texas

MARCH German submarines sink three American commercial ships submarine warfare

APRIL Congress declares war on Germany

MAY General John J. Pershing is named AEF Commander in Chief

JUNE General Pershing arrives in France

JUNE First AEF troops arrive in France

JULY 4 France cheers AEF troops as they parade through Paris

AUGUST War Gardens thrive in U.S.

SEPTEMBER Pershing moves AEF Headquarters from Paris to Chaumont near the front lines

OCTOBER First AEF unit has minor involvement with the enemy in Lorraine Sector of France

NOVEMBER U.S. creates the Signal Corps Pigeon Service

DECEMBER Checking the telephone lines

LOST STORIES OF THE GREAT WAR

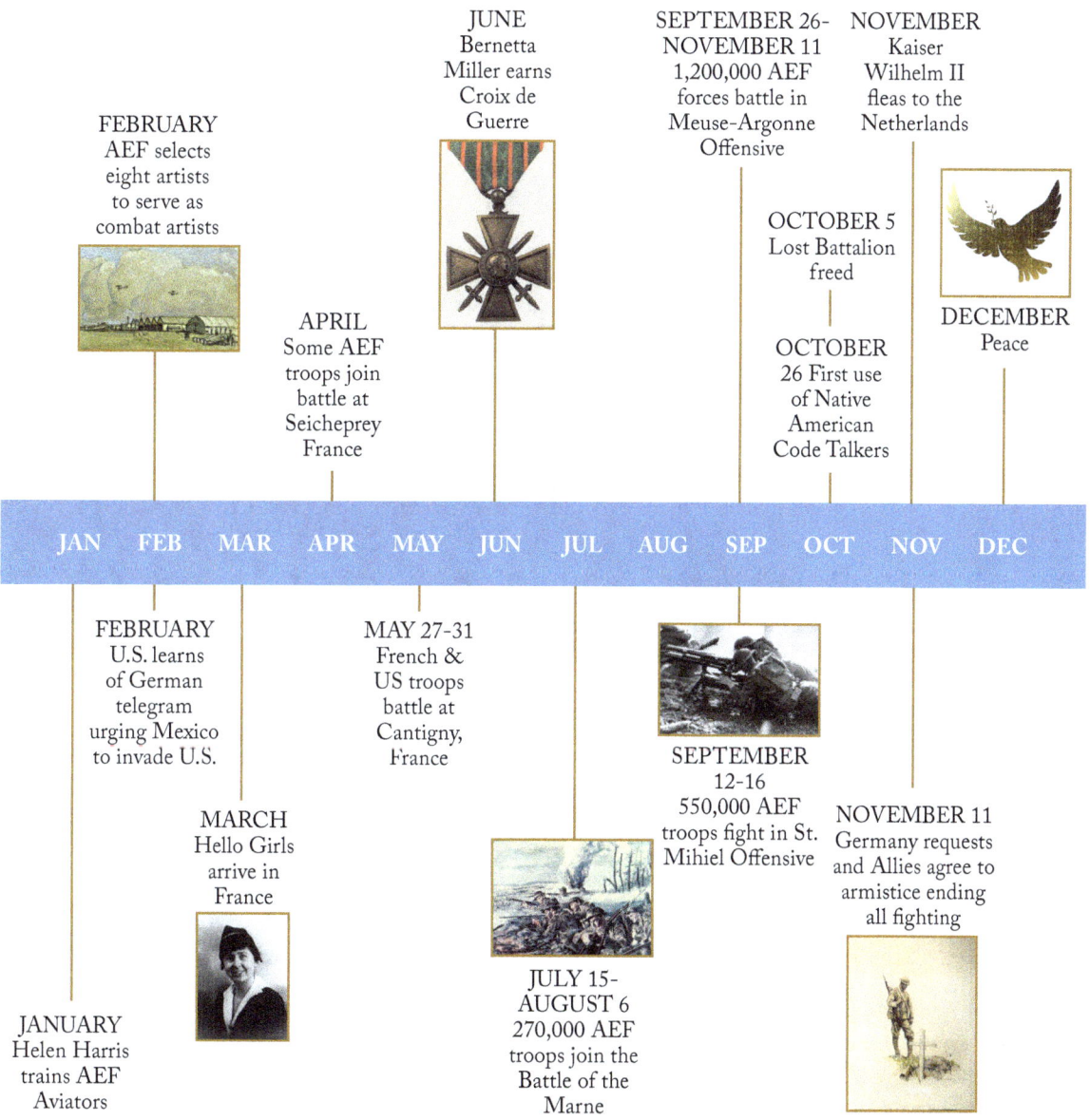

At the National World War I Museum and Memorial in Kansas City, Missouri, visitors cross a glass bridge suspended over a replicated Western Front poppy field. Nine thousand poppies, each representing one thousand deaths, stand for the nine million lives lost during the war. Courtesy Daderot Photography, National World War I Museum and Memorial via Wikimedia Commons.

Museums, Media, and Books

THE NATIONAL WWI MUSEUM AND MEMORIAL is a state-of-the-art museum dedicated to honoring those who served in the Great War. The museum preserves their history, shares their stories, and interprets the war and its impact on the global community. The original memorial opened to the public in 1926. A greatly expanded museum, completed in 2006, includes a recreated trench, a glass-bottomed bridge crossing over a field of poppies, and much more. Dozens of exhibits are available online at: www.theworldwar.org/explore/exhibitions/online-exhibitions. The National World War I Museum and Memorial is located at 2 Memorial Drive, Kansas City, Missouri.

NATIONAL WORLD WAR ONE MEMORIAL will be completed and dedicated in 2018. This outdoor space will honor the bravery of American forces during the Great War. The newly renovated and improved memorial will be rededicated on November 11, 2018, in celebration of the 100th Anniversary of the Armistice. The memorial is located at Pershing Park on Pennsylvania Avenue in Washington DC, about a block from the White House. Find more information at: https://www.nps.gov/nama/planyourvisit/national-world-war-i-memorial.htm

NATIONAL MUSEUM OF THE U.S. ARMY is scheduled to open in late 2019 in Fort Belvoir, Virginia. Interpretations of U.S. Army history and traditions will be offered. Additional information is available at http://thenmusa.org.

NATIONAL MUSEUM OF THE U.S. AIR FORCE features all types of aircraft, including Bleriot, Curtiss, and Nieuport planes as well as the 1909 Wright Military flyer. The museum is located on Wright Patterson Air Force Base near Dayton, Ohio. Online exhibits and videos can be examined at: www.nationalmuseum.af.mil.

FIRST DIVISION MUSEUM at Cantigny Park is dedicated to the 1st Infantry Division of the United States Army, called "The Big Red One." They were the first unit to deploy and engage in battle during WWI, WWII, and the Vietnam War. Established on June 8, 1917, the First Division has taken part in nearly every American War and is the longest continuously-serving division of the US Army. The museum is located within Cantigny Park at 1st 151 Winfield Road, Wheaton, IL. Explore online: www.Cantigny.org.

FIRST WORLD WAR WEBSITE includes multimedia presentations. Choose from numerous Great War topics. www.firstworldwar.com.

JEFFERSON BARRACKS HISTORIC SITE was a U.S. Army post from 1826 to 1946. Today the buildings are open to the public as museums with exhibits, educational programs, and displays of artifacts telling the history of the barracks. A Missouri Civil War Museum and a Telephone Museum are also located on the 426-acre site at 345 North Road, Saint Louis, MO. Learn more online: www.stlouisco.com/ParksandRecreation/ParkPages/JeffersonBarracks.

HISTORY CHANNEL offers a look at World War One through videos, speeches, photographs, and more. www.history.com/topics/world-war-i.

NEW HAMPSHIRE TELEPHONE MUSEUM houses the largest collection of antique telephones in New England. Visitors can explore over seven hundred examples of early telephones, switchboards, and switching equipment. Visit the museum at 22 East Main Street, Warner, NH, and at www.NHTelephoneMuseum.com.

PENNSYLVANIA MILITARY MUSEUM honors soldiers, sailors, airmen, and marines from Pennsylvania who have defended the state and the nation from 1747 to today. Exhibits, films, and programs concentrate on the roles of the individual servicemen and servicewomen. The museum is located at 51 Boal Avenue, Boalsburg, PA. For more information about programs, activities and tours, visit www.pamilmuseum.org.

PUBLIC BROADCASTING SERVICE, (PBS). View their film, The Great War and the Shaping of the 20th Century, at www.pbs.org/greatwar. PBS also presents written articles, films, and videos of the Great War and a multitude of other topics.

SMITHSONIAN AIR AND SPACE MUSEUM'S extensive collections include rare and significant aircraft and spacecraft from the original 1903 Wright Flyer to the Apollo 11 Command Module. The museum is located on the National Mall, Independence Avenue at 6th Street SW, Washington, DC. Or, visit online: www.airandspace.si.edu.

SPARK MUSEUM OF ELECTRICAL INVENTION features interactive exhibits and displays of inventions and innovations that changed the course of history. Visit at 1312 Bay Street, Bellingham, Washington, or online www.sparkmuseum.org.

TEXAS AIR MUSEUM is unique because it is dedicated to flight pioneers and the "golden-age" of aviation. Here you can learn more about the famous "Flying Stinson Family" and why San Antonio is considered the birthplace of American military aviation. See the Texas Air Museum at Stinson Field, 1234 99th Street, San Antonio, Texas. For additional information: www.texasairmuseum.org.

THE WRIGHT BROTHERS NATIONAL MEMORIAL in North Carolina marks the site where the brothers tested their flying machine. It includes outdoor monuments commemorating the first flight and marking its path, a bronze sculpture of the airplane, and a replica flyer used by park staff to demonstrate how the Wright brothers achieved flight. A Visitors Center includes exhibits and a bookstore. Check out the website at www.nps.gov/wrbr/index.htm. Or visit the memorial at 1401 National Park Drive, Mantes, North Carolina.

Recommended Reading

Adams, Simon. *Eyewitness World War I.* London: DK Publishing, 2014.

Freedman, Russell. *The War to End All Wars, World War I.* Boston: Sandpiper, 2010.

Hale, Nathan. *Treaties, Trenches, Mud, and Blood.* NY: Abrams, 2014.

Kenney, Karen L. *Everything World War I.* Washington DC: National Geographic Society, 2014.

Rasmussen, R. Kent. *World War I for Kids.* Chicago: Chicago Review Press, Incorporated, 2014.

Walsh, Barbara. *The Poppy Lady: Moina Belle Michael and Her Tribute to Veterans.* Honesdale, PA: Calkins Creek, 2016.

Zullo, Allen. *World War I Heroes.* NY: Scholastic, Inc., 2014.

Advanced Reading

Cornebise, Alfred Emile. *Art from the Trenches, America's Uniformed Artists in World War I.* College Station, TX: Texas A&M University Press, 1991.

Faulkner, Richard S. *Pershing's Crusaders, The American Soldier in World War I.* Lawrence, Kansas: University Press of Kansas, © 2017.

Hayter-Menzies, Grant. *From Stray Dog to World War Hero: The Paris Terrier Who Joined the First Division.* Lincoln, NE: University of Nebraska Press, Potomac Books imprint, 2015.

Kenney, Kimberly A. *Canton's Pioneers in Flight.* Charleston, SC: Arcadia Publishing, 2007.

Laplander, Robert J. *Finding the Lost Battalion, Beyond the Rumors, Myths and Legends of America's Famous WWI Epic.* Waterford, WI: The American Expeditionary Foundation, 2007.

Lebow, Eileen F. *Before Amelia, Women Pilots in the Early Days of Aviation.* Lincoln, NE: University of Nebraska Press, Potomac Books imprint, 2002.

Robinson, Gary. *The Language of Victory, American Indian Code Talkers.* Bloomington, IN: iUniverse LLC, 2014.

Educator Resources

NATIONAL ARCHIVES website promotes studying events and ideas of the past through primary document analysis. www.archives.gov/education/lessons.

NATIONAL EDUCATION ASSOCIATION'S lesson plans include multimedia resources that support historical studies of the Great War and the arts and literature it inspired. www.NEA.org/tools/lessons/60045.htm.

NATIONAL HISTORY DAY connects teachers and students to the best research and resources for teaching the Great War. NHD works with the National Archives and Records Administration, the Library of Congress, the Smithsonian National Museum of American History, the National World War I Museum and Memorial, and Army, Naval, and Marine Corps historical organizations to find rare primary sources. www.nhd.org/teaching-world-war-i.

NATIONAL PARK SERVICE offers lesson plans, materials, and activities on a large selection of subjects. Begin searching at www.NPS.gov/teachers/index.htm. One lesson plan, Chicago's Black Metropolis: Understanding History Through a Historic Place, looks at the neighborhood of the Fighting 8th and the Victory Monument pictured in Chapter 4 of this book. http://www.nps.gov/history/NR/twhp/wwwlps/lessons/53black/53black.htm.

NEW YORK TIMES provides Times articles, films, photographs, crosswords, and writing prompts to help students examine the cause, effect, and legacy of World War I. https://learning.blogs.nytimes.com/2014/09/10/teaching-world-war-i-with-the-new-york-times/

SMITHSONIAN FOR EDUCATORS offers many options for teachers, parents, and students to explore its wealth of treasures in the classroom or at home—topics range from the history of Native Americans to air and space travel. The site offers hundreds of innovative resources. https://www.si.edu/Educators.

WRIGHT BROTHERS NATIONAL MEMORIAL encourages educators to consider field trips. Stem-related curriculum materials and suggestions for further reading are offered online. www.nps.gov/wrbr/learn/education/classrooms/index.htm.

Source Notes

IMAGES

I gratefully acknowledge the significant contribution made to this book by the inclusion of historic images that speak louder than words. I offer sincerest thanks to the following persons and institutions who graciously permitted the use of their images.

Alamy, Inc.: 52, 57, 69, 72, 74, 98.

Karen Clarkson: 71.

Dover Publications, Inc.: 21, 111.

Library of Congress: Front Cover, 23 (all), 38, 50, 63, 64, Back Cover.

National Archives: 30, 35, 41, 43, 79, 81, 97, 102, 104, 115, 116.

National World War I Museum and Memorial: 44, 123.

New Hampshire Telephone Museum/photograph David Lauerman: 49.

John W. Nell/Historical Publishing Network, 77.

Science Photo Library: 32.

Scientific American Magazine: 24.

Shutterstock: 2, 8, 17, 108.

Smithsonian Institution/National Museum of American History/National Air & Space Museum: 82, 86, 89, 90, 91, 92, 93, 94, 95, 107, 112.

Wikimedia Commons: 10, 14, 15, 19, 26, 33, 37 (all), 47, 55, 60, 61, 68, 70, 101, 103, 106, 118, 120, 128.

Wikipedia: 84.

QUOTES

I wish to express my gratitude to the publishers listed below who generously permitted the use of quotes from their publications. These quotations, from voices of the past, have enriched and amplified the true stories recounted here. Heartfelt thanks to all!

CHAPTER ONE *The Great War*

"Homes that required a life-time to possess," William S. Braddan, Under Fire With the 370th Infantry AEF. (London: FB&C, Ltd., 2015). 69.

"No one who was not there can fully," John Ellis, Eye-Deep in Hell: Trench Warfare in World War I. (NY: Pantheon Books, Division of Random House, Inc., 1976). 51.

"A German flare shot up, broke into bright flame," Robert Graves. Good-Bye to All That. (London: Penguin Books, Ltd., 1929). 136.

"The train was a hospital train," John Lewis Barkley, Scarlet Fields: The Combat Memoir of a World War I Medal of Honor Hero. (Published by the University Press of Kansas, Lawrence, Kansas. © 2012). 57.

CHAPTER TWO *Telephone Linemen*

"In the morning the Americans get a concession," Abraham Lincoln Lavine, Circuits of Victory. (Garden City, NY: Doubleday, Page & Company, 1921. HardPress Publishing, Print Reproduction, no date). 306.

"We were chasing all the uniforms we saw," Lavine, 253.

"[We received] the most intense artillery fire the Division had seen," Frank Palmer Sibley, With the Yankee Division in France. (Boston: Little, Brown, and Company, 1919). 140.

"The enemy got pretty busy with their artillery," Lavine, 356-7.

"The St. Mihiel affair was a veritable nightmare," Lavine, 496, 507-508.

"Considering the masses of barb wire entanglements," John W. Nell, The Lost Battalion, A Private's Story. (San Antonio, TX: Historical Publishing Network, 2001). 64.

"One fine, clear, frosty day in the midst of firing, Observation Post No. 8," Lavine, 513.

"It would be unfair to close the record without speaking of," Sibley, 352.

"The officers and the men and the young women of the Signal Corps," Internet Archive, Final Report of Gen. John J. Pershing, Commander-in-Chief American Expeditionary Forces. (Washington D.C.: Government Printing Office, 1919). https://archive.org/stream/cu31924027816747#page/n0/mode/2up

CHAPTER THREE *Hello Girls*

"One night when Paris was under a rain of air bombs," Isaac Frederick Marcosson, S.O.S. America's Miracle in France. (NY: John Lane Company, 1919). 116.

"That first group of Signal Corp girls," Grace (Paddock) Banker, "I was a 'Hello Girl,'" Yankee Magazine, 1974. 68.

"[We] worked ten hours a day," Lettie Gavin, American Women in World War I. (Boulder, CO: The University Press of Colorado, 1997). 82.

"I reckon that the well-modulated," Lavine, 271.

"the troops pass, the artillery rumble by," Lavine, 493.

"We were rushed to death; we worked day and night," Lavine, 493.

"We were in an advance area," Lavine, 565.

"These funny old barracks proved to be fairly safe," Banker, 103.

"carried all the messages between the fighting units," Lavine, 565.

"The men and officers worked like mad," Banker, 105.

"This unit ... has performed invaluable service in handling," Lavine, 577.

"Their exceptional manner in discharging their duties," Lavine, 610.

CHAPTER FOUR *Fighting 8th*

"Fellows, you stand as pioneers on the frontier of your Race's," Braddan, 59.

"France is truly bled white as far as her manpower goes," Braddan, 52.

"In those short minutes of rest, I'd look around at the country," Barkley, 59-61.

"the true democratic spirit, catering alike to all," Richard S. Faulkner, Pershing's Crusaders: The American Soldier in World War I. (Published by the University Press of Kansas, Lawrence, KS, © 2017). www.kansaspress.ku.edu. Used by permission of the publisher. 206.

"[The French] treated us with respect," Faulkner, 209.

"France will always be looked upon by the American Negros," Faulkner, 209.

"modernism, cleanliness, and morals," Faulkner, 209.

"Take it from me it is a good thing for us," Faulkner, 196.

"understand why Americans should treat one another so harshly," Faulkner, 208.

"gentle folks of Lorraine who welcomed us," Braddan, 51.

"ignorant of ordinary politeness, and wild," Faulkner, 152.

"For days inhabitants have been evacuating," Braddan, 77.

"It's a safe bet that when you receive this," Braddan, 84.

"Beginning September 27, 1918, we sailed into them," Emmitt J. Scott, The American Negro in the World War, Chapter XV, Awards and Commendations. http://net.lib.byu.edu/estu/wwi/comment/scott/ScottTC.htm.

"Just before three [AM] the air was split," Peixotto, Ernest, The American Front (1919). (NY: Charles Scribner's Sons, 1919). 161-163.

"The men were barefooted, ragged, and lousy," Braddan, 93.

"I cannot commend too highly the spirit," Scott, Preface.

"You, [the 370th Regiment] have given us your best and," Braddan, 101.

CHAPTER FIVE *Code Talkers*

"I was born here in America," Thomas A. Britten, American Indians in World War I. (Albuquerque, NM: University of New Mexico Press, 1997). 64.

"The need for care in telephoning was impressed on us," Sibley, 68.

"There was every reason to believe every," Bloor, Colonel A. W., U.S. Army Memo, January 23, 1919.

"The enemy's complete surprise is evidence," Bloor.

"I felt no American could be or should be better than the first Americans," Britten, 76.

"The North American Indian took his place," Britten, 183.

CHAPTER SIX *Carrier Pigeons*

"There has long been a controversy among pigeon breeders," The New Country Life, August, 1918.

"It was terrible," Nell, 70-72.

"There are no words to depict the terrible conditions," Nell, 89.

"I was still carrying an old broken hoe I had picked up," Nell, 90.

"under such constant strain and fear," Nell, 83.

"A barrage came plowing its way down the hill," Nell, 94.

"We knew without a doubt that this was our last," Nell, 95.

"It was like being reborn," Nell, 98.

"died gloriously for their country," Nell, 121.

CHAPTER SEVEN *Combat Artists*

"The war artist puts on a steel helmet," National Museum of the U.S. Army, http://thenmusa.org/into-the-trenches.php.

"I had just gotten well into a drawing," Harvey Everett Townsend, War Diary of a Combat Artist, (Boulder, CO: University Press of Colorado, 1991). 67.

"the usual problems of one's craft," Cornebise, Emile Alfred, Art from the Trenches, (College Station, TX: Texas A&M University Press, 1991). 34.

"As my father was a ship builder," Cornebise, 12.

"sparkles enchantingly against its sunny," Cornebise, 14.

"the character of the struggle and the men engaged." Cornebise, 35.

"Rain and slush; mud and dirt; my paper wet," Peixotto, 176.

"without resorting to sensational tricks and fakes." Cornebise, 29.

"Just before dawn [December 13, 1918]," Peixotto, 226-227.

CHAPTER EIGHT *Flying Schoolgirls*

"The pilot sat out in front (and not strapped in!) with nothing," Kenney, Kimberly A., Canton's Pioneers in Flight. (Charleston, SC: Arcadia Publishing, 2007). 106.

"If you are going to let other people decide," Lebow, Eileen F., reproduced from Before Amelia, Women Pilots in the Early Days of Aviation, by permission of the University of Nebraska Press. Copyright 2002 by Potomac Books, Inc. 200.

"so surely could a man." Kenney, 106.

"I wouldn't say I had a rough time," Kenney, 109.

"There is an indescribable," Pilot Stories: Ruth Law, National Postal Museum, Smithsonian, https://postalmuseum.si.airmail/pilot/pilot_female/pilot_female_law.html. Originally published in the Christian Science Monitor, May 26, 1917, "Women as Aviators." Public Domain.

CHAPTER NINE *Peace*

"As the hour approached, officers and men of the artillery," Sibley, 340-341.

"We went back to our old quarters that night," Barkley, 215.

"celebrate in some small way," Gavin, 91.

"As the darkness grew thicker, the hoarded fireworks," Sibley, 341.

"At 4:30 PM every church bell in France began to ring," Gavin, 91.

"A frenzy of joy sweeps over," Lavine, xiv.

"The news [of the armistice] sent me out walking alone," Graves, 347.

"The very thought of engaging in another war should be bitterly," Nell, 117.

"The memory of the unflinching fortitude," Internet Archive, Final Report of Gen. John J. Pershing, Commander-in-Chief American Expeditionary Forces. (Washington D.C.: Government Printing Office, 1919). https://archive.org/stream/cu31924027816747#page/n0/mode/2up

"All of a sudden I heard my name called." Barkley, 219-221.

Selected Bibliography

Arthur, Max, Ed. *Forgotten Voices of the Great War, Told by Those Who Were There.* London: Ebury Press, 2002.

Banker, Grace, courtesy of Merle Egan. "I was a 'Hello Girl," *Yankee Magazine.* March 1974.

Barbeau, Arthur E. & Florette Henri. *The Unknown Soldiers, African-American Troops in World War I.* Philadelphia: Temple University Press, 1974.

Barkley, John Lewis. *Scarlet Fields: The Combat Memoir of a World War I Medal of Honor Hero.* Published by the University Press of Kansas, Lawrence, Kansas, © 2012. www.kansaspress.ku.edu. Used by permission of the publisher.

Bloor, Colonel A. W. Bloor. "Transmitting Messages in Choctaw," *U.S. Army Memo to Commanding General of the Thirty-Sixth Division,* January 23, 1919.

Braddan, William S. *Under Fire With the 370th Infantry AEF.* London: Forgotten Books, a registered trademark of FB&c, Ltd., 2015.

Britten, Thomas A. *American Indians in World War I, at War and at Home.* Albuquerque, NM: University of New Mexico Press, 1997.

Buckley, Gail. American Patriots, *The Story of Blacks in the Military from the Revolution to Desert Storm.* NY: Random House Trade Paperbacks, 2001.

Carroll, Andrew. *My Fellow Soldiers, General John Pershing and the Americans Who Helped Win the Great War.* NY: Penguin Press, 2017.

Christian Science Monitor, "Women as Aviators." Boston: Mary Baker Eddy, Publisher, May 26, 1917, 22.

Cobbs, Elizabeth. *The Hello Girls, America's First Women Soldiers.* Cambridge, Massachusetts: Harvard University Press, 2017.

Cornebise, Alfred Emile. *Art from the Trenches, America's Uniformed Artists in World War I.* College Station, TX: Texas A&M University Press, 1991.

Dobbins, James & Robert Zoelick. *Foreign Service: Five Decades on the Frontlines of American Diplomacy.* Washington DC: Brookings Institution Press, 2017.

Doughboy Center, *The Story of the American Expeditionary Forces,* Joseph Oklahombi Choctaw, Doughboy, *Code Talker, and Mighty Warrior,* U.S. 36th Infantry Division. www.worldwar1.com/dbc/j_oklah.htm.

Ellis, John & Michael Cox. T*he World War I Databook, The Essential Facts and Figures for all the Combatants.* London: Aurum Press Ltd., 1993.

Ellis, John. *Eye Deep in Hell, Trench Warfare in World War I.* NY: Pantheon Books, a division of Random House, Inc., 1976.

Freidel, Frank. *Over There, the Story of America's First Great Overseas Crusade.* NY: McGraw-Hill Publishing Company, 1964.

Faulkner, Richard S. Pershing's Crusaders, *The American Soldier in World War I.* Published by the University Press of Kansas, Lawrence, Kansas, © 2017. www.kansaspress.ku.edu. Used by permission of the publisher.

Gavin, Lettie. *American Women in World War I, They Also Served.* Boulder, CO: The University Press of Colorado, 1997.

Graves, Robert. *Good-Bye to All That, an Autobiography.* London: Penguin Books, Ltd., 1929.

Hartley and Sons. *Belgian Homing Pigeons: Their Rearing, Training and Management.* Reprint of a book originally published in 1884 book. The publication is within the Public Domain.

Haskin, Eleanor, Ed. *Independent Telephony in New England, a History 1876-1976.* Burlington, VT: George Little Press, 1976.

Hayter-Menzies, Grant, *From Stray Dog to World War Hero: The Paris Terrier Who Joined the First Division.* Lincoln, NE: University of Nebraska Press, Potomac Books imprint, 2015.

Hemingway, Ernest, Intro and Ed. *Men At War: The Best War Stories of all Time.* NY, NY: Wings Books, 1991.

Internet Archive. *Final Report of Gen. John J. Pershing, Commander-in-Chief American Expeditionary Forces.* Washington, D.C.: Government Printing Office, 1919. https://archive.org.

Irwin. Julia F. *Making the World Safe, The American Red Cross and a Nation's Humanitarian Awakening.* NY: Oxford University Press, 2013.

Kenney, Kimberly A. *Canton's Pioneers in Flight.* Charleston, SC: Arcadia Publishing, 2007.

Laplander, Robert J. *Finding the Lost Battalion, Beyond the Rumors, Myths and Legends of America's Famous WWI Epic.* Waterford, WI: American Expeditionary Foundation, 2007.

Lavine, Abraham Lincoln. *Circuits of Victory.* Garden City, NY: Doubleday, Page & Company, 1921. HardPress Publishing, Print Reproduction, no date.

Lebow, Eileen F. Before Amelia, *Women Pilots in the Early Days of Aviation*. Reproduced text by permission of the University of Nebraska Press, Lincoln, NE. Copyright 2002 by Potomac Books, Inc.

Marcosson, Isaac Frederick. S.O.S. *America's Miracle in France*. NY: John Lane Company, 1919.

Marrin, Albert. *The Yanks Are Coming*. NY: Atheneum, 1989.

Miller, Arthur P., Jr., and Marjorie L. Miller. *Pennsylvania Military Museum*. Mechanicsburg, Pennsylvania: Stackpole Books, 2005.

National Museum of the United States Army. http://thenmusa.org/into-the-trenches.php.

National Postal Museum, Smithsonian Institution, "Pilot Stories: Ruth Law." http://postalmuseum.si.edu/airmail/pilot/pilot/_female/pilot_female_law.html. .

Nell, John W. The Lost Battalion, *A Private's Story*. San Antonio, TX: Historical Publishing Network, 2001.

Peixotto, Ernest. *The American Front (1919)*. NY: Charles Scribner's Sons, 1919.

Pershing, General John J. *My Experiences in the First World War*. NY: HarperCollins Publishers, 1931.

Raines, Rebecca Robbins. *Getting the Message Through, A Branch History of the U.S. Army Signal Corps*. Washington D.C.: Center of Military History, United States Army, 1996.

Robinson, Gary. *The Language of Victory, American Indian Code Talkers of World War I and World War II*. Bloomington, IN: iUniverse, LLC, 2014.

Rohan, Jack. *Rags: The Story of a Dog Who Went to War*. NY: Grosset & Dunlap Publishers by arrangement with Harper & Brothers, 1930.

Schneider, Dorothy and Carl J. *Into the Breach: American Women Overseas in World War I*. NY: Viking Penguin, 1991.

Scientific American, "The Telephone in Khaki." NY: Munn & Co., Inc., Publishers, 1918, 252.

Scott, Emmitt J., *The American Negro in the World War*, Chapter XV, Awards and Commendations. http://net.lib.byu.edu/estu/wwi/comment/scott/ScottTC.htm.

Sibley, Frank Palmer. *With the Yankee Division in France – Primary Source Edition*. Boston: Little, Brown, and Company, 1919.

Smith, Page. *America Enters the World: A People's History of the Progressive Era and World War I*. NY: McGraw-Hill Book Company, 1985.

Tegetmeier, W. B. *The Homing or Carrier Pigeon, Its History, General Management, and Method of Training.* London: George Routledge and Sons, 1871.

"The Telephone in Khaki." *Scientific American Magazine.* March 23, 1918.

Terraine, John. White Heat, *The New Warfare 1914-1918.* London: Leo Cooper, 1992.

Townsend, Harvey Everett. *War Diary of a Combat Artist.* Boulder, CO: University Press of Colorado, 1991.

Twain, Mark (Samuel Clemens). *A Connecticut Yankee in King Arthur's Court.* NY: Charles L. Webster and Company, 1889, 177. www.gutenberg.net..

Wells, H. G., *The War in the Air,* Chapter IV. The Free Library by Farlex.

Western Front Association. "The 370th Infantry—Chicago's 8th Illinois National Guard in WW1." www.westernfrontassociation.com/the-great-war/great-war-on-land/other-war-theatres.html.

Wilson, Woodrow. "Joint Address to Congress Leading to a Declaration of War Against Germany (1917)." *U.S. National Archives & Records Administration.* www.ourdocuments.gov.

"WWI Choctaw Indian Code Talkers" and "American Heroes," www.TexasMilitaryForcesMuseum.org//choctaw/codetalkers.htm.

Yockelson, Mitchell. *Forty-Seven Days, How Pershing's Warriors came of Age to Defeat the German Army in World War I.* NY: New American Library, 2016.

Zeiger, Susan. *In Uncle Sam's Service.* Ithaca, NY: Cornell University Press, 1999.

Zullo, Allan. *World War I Heroes,* 10 True Tales. NY: Scholastic, Inc., 2014.

www.ingramcontent.com/pod-product-compliance
Lightning Source LLC
Chambersburg PA
CBHW060529010526
44110CB00052B/2537